OWLS

Journeys around the world

OWLS

Journeys around the world

David Hollands

BLOOMINGS
BOOKS

For Bill Flentje, Eric Forsman, Hans Frey, Richard Hill,
Denver Holt, Rod Kavanagh, Pertti Saurola, Fred Söllner,
Peter Steyn, Sumio Yamamoto, John Young and my many
other owling friends around the world.

Contents

vi Acknowledgments
viii Foreword *by Rod Kavanagh*
1 Introduction

The Journeys

7 **England**
Barn Owl

13 **Alaska, USA**
Snowy Owl

45 **Argentina**
Burrowing Owl

57 **Austria**
Eagle Owl • Long-Eared Owl

81 **Christmas Island**
Christmas Island Hawk Owl

99 **Costa Rica**
Spectacled Owl • Ferruginous Pygmy Owl • Pacific Screech Owl

113 **Finland**
Ural Owl • European Pygmy Owl
• Tengmalm's Owl • Great Grey Owl

141 **Japan**
Blakiston's Fish Owl

163 **Oregon, USA**
Spotted Owl

177 **Queensland, Australia**
Lesser Sooty Owl • Rufous Owl

201 **South Africa**
White-Faced Scops Owl • Spotted Eagle Owl • Verreaux's Eagle Owl

213 **Victoria, Australia**
Powerful Owl

233 **The Future - Do owls have one?**
236 **Further Reading**
238 **Index**

Acknowledgements

All journeys involve people and I have been fortunate to meet many, making a lot of new friends and seeing many old ones. Without them, my quest would have been impossible.

In Finland, I developed a wonderful friendship with Pertti Saurola and his wife Hemuli. Before my first visit there, I had met Pertti only once and Hemuli not at all but they welcomed Margaret and me like royalty, lending us their house, taking us to a succession of Ural Owl sites and repeatedly showing gestures of kindness and warmth. Pertti's friend Pekka Pouttu was also a great help, spending long hours on frosty nights helping me with Pygmy Owls and taking me to meet the Capercaillie which considered itself his rival.

Wolfgang and Petja Baumgart in Berlin have been our friends for a long time. They were not directly involved with the Eagle Owls but came all the way to Vienna to introduce me to Hans Frey there. Through Hans, this then led on to my meeting Fred Söllner and his family. All gave me unstinting help and hospitality and, after two visits to Austria, I have come close to being one of the Söllner family. Fred has also generously allowed me to use two of his fine Eagle Owl shots in the book.

One of the earliest journeys was to South Africa with old friends Peter and Jenny Steyn. Peter is a fine photographer himself and a great owl man and gave us a memorable trip from the Cape to the Kalahari, then introduced us to Mike and Liz Jankowitz, who became firm friends and later took us to the Kruger Park.

Argentina was a brief trip but I am grateful to my son Richard, a resident there at the time, who first spotted the Burrowing Owls and introduced me to Gustavo Ranovsky who made it possible for me to photograph them.

In Costa Rica, I had two professional guides, Agustin Zuniga and Demetrio. I never learned Demetrio's surname but his knowledge of the local birds was superb.

Eric Forsman is a world expert on Spotted Owls. Margaret and I visited him for just one superb day in Oregon, struggling up and down steep forest slopes together with his colleague Pete Loschl.

Denver Holt knows more about Snowy Owls than almost anyone. For years we never met, while I bombarded him with e-mails and he sent me vital information about the owls. Finally, in 2003, our Alaskan visits coincided and we were able to convert correspondence into friendship. In 1999, I also had much help from Julie Petersen, Denver's assistant there and then, in 2003, from Julie's successor, Pete Seidensticker. Another Alaskan correspondent was Robert Suydam, a resident biologist in

PREVIOUS PAGES
TITLE PAGE
The Essence of owls. Two Powerful Owls roosting in the rain. Victoria, Australia 2004
CONTENTS PAGE
Attacking Snowy Owl. A male bird diving straight at the author's head.

Barrow, who would always send me priceless assessments of the situation there.

I had never dared hope that I would ever see Blakiston's Fish Owl but this came about in Japan through the help and friendship of Sumio Yamamoto and his wife Akiko who gave up a complete week to ensure that I spent every possible moment with the owls.

In Australia, I have many people to thank. On Christmas Island, Richard Hill was studying the hawk owl and I would never have found it without his help.

The Powerful Owl has been a passion for many years and Bill Flentje has been my companion throughout. We have spent many cold nights in the forest together and his wife Betty and son Neil were always there to provide sustenance and help with towers.

John Young and I have made more expeditions together than I can remember. He is, quite simply, the most remarkable naturalist whom I have ever known. The Rufous and Lesser Sooty Owl nests were both his and I watched them from his hides, built with extraordinary skill and courage, high in the trees of the rainforest. His wife, Junell, did not climb to the hides but always provided welcome hospitality when we came down to the earthbound world.

Alan Cowan is a great friend and has been with me to both Alaska and Japan, accompanied, on the Alaskan trip, by his wife, Susan. He has great patience and tolerance, helping me to put up hides, seeing me in and waiting for long hours, always in the cold, until I have been ready to come out.

Not all help has been in the field. After a long period of gestation, there follows the birth and I have had two excellent midwives. Warwick Forge, my publisher, has shown enthusiasm, dedication, tolerance and initiative and it would have been very hard to produce the book without him. It would certainly have been a very different book without my designer Danie Pout. She has wonderful flair and originality and has been able to make more of my text and pictures than I could ever have dreamed of.

I am very happy, too, that Rod Kavanagh has agreed to provide a foreword. Rod is Australia's leading owl researcher, a scientist with an international reputation, who has always retained the common touch and an ability to see the natural world with the same enthusiasm and wonder as the amateur.

Finally, there is my own family. Richard I have mentioned and my daughters, Louise and Sarah, have looked on their father's antics with a mixture of interest and amusement but always with great support. Last of all, there is my wife, Margaret, who has been with me on almost every trip outside Australia. She is not an owl expert and would probably not have selected some of the destinations but, without her, I would have been lost and this project would never have gone ahead.

To all of these people, I say "Thank you". I hope that the end result will have justified their efforts.

Foreword

David Hollands has realised his calling to adventure photography! Somehow, around the demands of his busy medical practice, David's passion for owls has taken him to many parts of Australia, and now to the world, in his pursuit of the compelling images which capture the essence of these magnificent and mysterious creatures. David's exquisite portrayal of owls in their natural environment has done much to raise public awareness of these birds and their conservation needs, especially in Australia.

Owl photography is an adventure; one full of uncertainties, frustrations and great delights. Being primarily nocturnal and usually wide ranging, there are no guarantees that an owl can even be located in its natural habitat, let alone photographed. Part of David's adventure has been the lasting friendships he has made with many owl enthusiasts and researchers from around the world who have assisted him in his quest by taking him to the favourite haunts of these elusive birds. Just getting there has often been a physical ordeal in itself. Owls occupy a wide range of environments from tall, mountain forests, through vine thickets and rainforest to drier woodlands and grassland at all elevations and in tropical, temperate and arctic latitudes. Accessing many of these often remote areas at night, when the birds are active, presents a significant challenge to anyone. To then climb up the 20-30 metres needed to get level with the owls in their treetop habitat takes a particular level of dedication and stamina. This, before even one photograph is taken, is a measure of the absorbing fascination that the owls hold for David and for others who have had the privilege of observing them in the wild.

But, succeed he does. David Hollands' first book about owls "Birds of the Night", published in 1991, is a masterpiece of photography and narrative that has done more than any other work to bring home to Australians the magic of our own unique owl species. He has followed the pioneering steps of the great Australian naturalist and writer, David Fleay, in presenting important, accurate information about owl biology, habitat and behaviour in a thoroughly gripping and entertaining manner. In this latest adventure, subtitled "Journeys Around the World", David continues to combine his field natural history skills, exceptional photography and evocative writing to highlight and expose some of the world's most interesting owls.

Twenty-one owls from six continents form the subject of this book. David's selection includes many lesser known owls, such as the tropical owls of Costa Rica (including the spectacular Spectacled Owl), and threatened species (including Blakiston's Fish Owl and the Christmas Island Hawk Owl), along with other widespread and familiar species (including the Barn Owl, which is always beautiful no matter how many times one is seen or photographed). Closer to my heart, David has also featured what must be one of the most impressive of all the world's owls, the majestic and regal Powerful Owl of Australia's tall east coast forests.

David's prognosis for the future of owls in many parts of the world is bleak, and this is a sad reflection about the future of much of our biota because owls, as top predators, have a capacity to provide early warning of adverse environmental changes. Indeed, David lists many of the threatening processes currently acting upon owls and it is up to us, collectively, to recognise these threats and to carefully plan for their amelioration. Significant advances have been made in some areas, but we need to maintain our vigilance and to increase our awareness of these issues. This book displays to us the joy of owls but it also stimulates us to work together for their conservation worldwide.

Rod Kavanagh
Sydney, Australia
July, 2004

Dr Rod Kavanagh is Principal Research Scientist with the State Forests of New South Wales and has worked for many years on the study and conservation of Australia's large forest owls.

Introduction

I have a passion for owls. It has been there for longer than I can remember and shows no sign of going away. Some of my friends regard it as a disease or an obscure form of insanity and there seems no doubt that, once caught, the condition is lifelong and incurable. Surely no normal man would forsake his bed to spend his nights in the darkness of the forest, listening for a sound which might never come at all.

It is not hard to become entranced by owls. There is an aura about them, which no other birds possess. Their very ability to operate in the theatre of darkness ensures this. It is a foreign medium for man and the owls' capacity to be at home in it at once imparts an air of mystery. Their calls enhance the atmosphere; eerie hoots and fearful screams, often sounding without warning in the silence of the night.

Owls are hard to spot but any sighting only adds to an air of the supernatural; the blackened shadow across the night sky; the ghostly white wraith, passing for a moment through the gleam of headlights; the red glow of eyes in the beam of a spotlight. Other night birds may have some of these features but owls too have a face with forward pointing eyes, adding human appeal to the air of mystery. Small wonder that they have evoked both fear and fascination among people.

That fascination led me to a study of the owls of Australia. For nearly ten years I used every moment that I could spare to find, watch, listen and photograph all the Australian species. It seemed apt to call the resulting book "Birds of the Night", in part a tribute to my friend Eric Hosking, father of British bird photography, whose book of the same name on British owls had inspired me over 40 years before.

With "Birds of the Night" complete, I took stock. My obsession with owls was insatiable and there was a world of owls that I did not know. I had to see more. Perhaps I could make a series of expeditions to other countries to try to study their owls. In Australia, I had been able to use tall towers and hides built high in trees. Overseas, there would be no access to these but perhaps, through careful selection, I could find owls which I could see and photograph from lesser heights.

So began a personal odyssey, which will never be complete. It was a project without boundaries whose main limiting factors were luck and time. I have had a

lot of very good luck but, even after 12 years, there has never been enough time.

It has led me from the Equator to the Arctic and to every continent along the way. I have seen pristine wilderness and ravaged landscapes. I have seen a multitude of plants, animals and birds as well as the owls. I have met many people and made many friends. Often I have been sidetracked but the overall focus has always been on owls.

It has been a journey both of wonder and of learning. There have been nights of sheer magic and nights of total emptiness. I have learned much but I am not the only owl fanatic and I have seen the outstanding work of people who are much more expert than I am. I have realised too how much remains unknown. There are no quick answers with owls and there are species which may be close to extinction and yet whose nests have never been described.

This is not a scientific book. Any contribution that I may have made to owl knowledge is small. It is a personal story of my journeys to discover the wonder, the variety and the fascination of owls. Mankind has not always treated them kindly and anything which might turn the tide slightly in their favour is surely worthwhile?

FAR LEFT
Snowy Owl arriving at nest with Lemming.
LEFT
The Female Spotted Eagle Owl allowed me to climb almost into her nest to take her picture.

Alaska U.S.A.

ENGLAND

Oregon U.S.A.

COSTA RICA

ARGENTINA

FINLAND

AUSTRIA

Hokkaido JAPAN

CHRISTMAS ISLAND

Queensland AUSTRALIA

SOUTH AFRICA

Victoria AUSTRALIA

The Journeys

England

Barn Owl

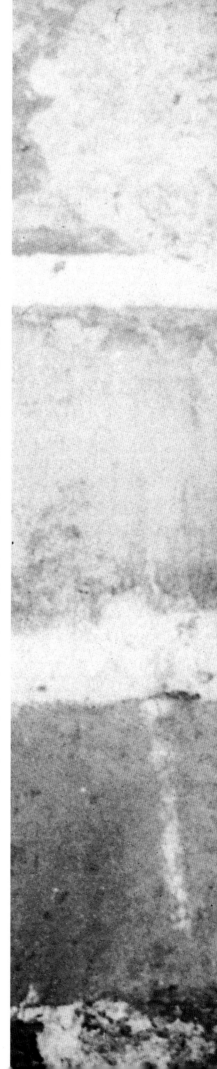

It was the English Barn Owls which started it all, over forty years ago. This was not really a true journey, for they lived only a short distance from my home at that time, but they were my first owls and they sparked off a fascination which I would carry for life.

I had sometimes seen Barn Owls there in previous years, gliding low over the frosty fields of Warwickshire in the dim light of a winter's afternoon. They appeared like wraiths, as if from nowhere, and vanished into the gloom, giving me no clue to either their origin or their destination. It was a chance meeting with a farmer one spring which produced the answer. He told me of the white owl which he often saw over his farmyard and which he suspected might be living in one of his barns.

There is a profusion of barns on English farms, many of them made of brick or stone and of great age. They were built at a time when the farmers probably had a closer affinity with nature than they have today and some of them had attic lofts with a floor and a gap in the wall, made specially for owls to enter. The farmers knew who their friends were. This was such a barn with brick walls and a tiled roof. Below the gable, there were two holes where the brickwork had not been completed. It looked promising.

There was a small trapdoor in the floor of the loft. It had not been opened for years. I climbed to it, pushed it up and, above the sound of creaking hinges and falling debris, came a noise like steam from an exhaust valve.

The owl was backed into one corner of the little loft, wings half spread, bill open and hissing. In years to come, I would come to know that sound as well as my own voice but that was the first time that I had ever heard it and the effect was electrifying. Around her, the floor was heaped with the accumulated pellets of many years and, at her feet, were five white eggs. I lowered the trap door and left her.

Three weeks later, I was ready to start. It was not hard to screen off a corner of the loft so that I could climb in unseen; unseen but not undetected, for my arrival was invariably greeted by a chorus of hissing from the four young. No doubt the female heard me coming too for, after that initial visit, she had always left the loft by the time that I entered.

Much has changed in forty years. My camera was a Thornton Pickard, a handcrafted instrument of polished wood, brass knobs and canvas bellows, taking pictures on 5 X 4 inch glass plates. I had holders for only eight plates and, when these had been exposed, it was time to go home. The camera had the advantage of being almost silent but the same could not be said for the single-use flash bulbs, which went off with a miniature explosion. It was a slow and cumbersome set-up but, within its limitations, capable of producing quality pictures, all, of course, in black and white.

I waited for night and for the adults to come. Inside the loft, it was inky black but there was still a square of faint light through the gap in the brickwork. From outside, I heard the hissing scream of a returning owl while the owlets hissed back in anticipation. Then the light in the brickwork was blocked out. For a few moments, the owl waited and then the light returned and I heard scuffling footsteps across the floor. The owlets hisses were joined by a gurgling sound as the first of them was fed.

Then I pressed the shutter release. In that confined space, the light was blinding and, when my eyes recovered, the owl had gone. This was as well for my next task was to put my hand outside the hide to change the flash bulb.

After such a cataclysm, I fully expected the owls to be gone for the night but, in a short time, the female was back. Next time I fired the flash, she was away for only a few minutes and, after that, she ignored it. Not so with any sound on my part and I had only to brush a hand against my clothing to elicit a chorus of hissing from both adults and owlets. A Barn Owl's hearing is very sensitive.

Once the female had lost her fear of the flash, she remained with the young and the male brought the food to her, entering through the hole in the brickwork, usually with a rat. He stayed only long enough to transfer the prey and was gone, screaming as he flew out over the farmyard.

I had time for only two sessions in the hide. On the first visit, the young were little powder-puff balls of white down. By the next time, they were almost ready to fly, fully-feathered with their down nearly all gone. As I came to the barn, one stood in the gap in the brickwork, looking out on the world which it would soon join. I never saw them again.

Since those days, there have been great changes for British Barn Owls. Much of the rough pasture, favoured for hunting by the owls, has gone under the plough. Rodent populations have dropped and the owls themselves have fallen victim to agricultural poisons. Hollow nest trees have blown down or been felled and many of the favoured barns have been knocked down or converted into dwellings. It is a sad commentary on modern times and the owls have suffered but there is a realisation of the problems and, hopefully, the fall in their numbers will be stemmed.

Whether or not my barn still stands with its resident owls, I shall probably never know, but the memory of those first ever sessions with an owl in the darkness remains as vivid as on the nights when I was there.

PREVIOUS PAGE
The only way into the barn was through a small gap in the brickwork
OPPOSITE, TOP
The English Barn Owl that began it all. Female with 5 small chicks. Warwickshire 1961
OPPOSITE, BOTTOM
Arriving with a Brown Rat, the male hesitated, perhaps sensing that, for the first time, my hide was occupied.

Alaska

USA

Snowy Owl

The E-mail sounded promising: Wednesday January 13th 1999 *"David, I understand people are seeing Lemmings already in Barrow. Given that the owls have not bred for the last two seasons, I think we have a good chance. Keep in touch. Denver."*

That was the message that I had been waiting for. It was still very early in the season but the signs were promising.

The Snowy Owl! The great white owl of the Arctic! For as long as I can remember, I have been fascinated by this almost mythical bird which lives in one of the most inhospitable places on earth. For years, I thought of it as an unachievable fantasy, a bird to read about alongside tales of wolves, bears, and arctic explorers but one which I was never likely to see.

To start with, there was the problem of getting there. Almost its entire breeding range lies above the Arctic circle; Arctic Russia, Lapland, northern Alaska, Arctic Canada and northern Greenland, all places which seemed beyond the reach of the ordinary traveller.

Then there were the habits of the bird itself; highly nomadic and with a breeding season which goes in cycles of anything from two to four years, mirroring the cycle of its' principal prey, the lemming. It is almost totally dependent on these arctic rodents to sustain it through the breeding season and, if there are no lemmings, there are few owls and no breeding. For anybody wanting to find Snowy Owls, this information is vital and I knew of no one who could give it to me. It seemed that my Snowy Owls were never going to progress beyond a dream.

However, it was a dream which would not go away. I visited Finland, where my friend Pertti Saurola had occasionally seen Snowies in northern Lapland. In 1995, another friend saw them in abundance in Kamchatka while on an international shorebird expedition across the top of Russia. Surely there was a way for me to find these birds within the limitations of my own resources?

Slowly the clues began to appear and Barrow, at the northernmost point in Alaska, seemed to be the key. It is remote but does have an air service, there are places to stay and there are roads running in three directions for a short distance around the village. Most importantly, there are a number of records of the owls having bred there.

In 1996, I made contact with Robert Suydam, a wildlife biologist based in Barrow, and then, the following year, with Denver Holt from Montana who comes to Barrow every year to study the Snowy Owls. Both were enormously friendly and helpful to me and my web of spies was starting to take shape.

1996 was an excellent year for Snowy Owls but, by the time I found out, it was too late, the young were flying and the short arctic summer was coming to an end. That had been the second consecutive good lemming year and it was too much to expect that there would be three in a row. There weren't. In 1997 there were a few owls about in the spring but no breeding and the picture in 1998 was much the same.

Of course, in any one year, there are always Snowy Owls breeding somewhere. Unlike many migrants, which fly from north to south, or the nomadic birds of inland Australia, which may wait years for a good season, Snowy Owls are circumpolar, traversing the high arctic latitudes to find somewhere where there is an abundance of lemmings. Sometimes it will be Alaska but it may just as well be Canada, Greenland, Lapland or arctic Russia. In each place, the lemmings are cyclical but the cycles are not all in step together and, somewhere, there will always be a summer with lemmings and that is where the Snowy Owls will go. The owl which breeds in Barrow one year may nest in Kamchatka the next.

And so to 1999. Denver Holt's report of lemmings in January was promising but it was still mid-winter and a lot could happen between then and the spring. I rang a friend in Anchorage in southern Alaska. The temperature outside was −45° Fahrenheit and an icy wind blew through the blackness of the long arctic night. It would be a long time before there was any sign of the owls coming back. However, my plans had to be made well in advance and I resolved to go. Margaret and I would go together and we would be joined by two old friends, Alan and Susan Cowan.

Barrow! That is the English name but the Inupiat eskimos have lived there for four thousand years and they have their own name for it, "UKPIAGVIK", "The place for hunting Snowy Owls." I hoped that they had not hunted too many of them.

We arrived on June 6th, flying north from Anchorage over the spectacularly beautiful Alaskan landscape; dark green boreal forest, icy blue lakes and the jagged snow capped mountain peaks, first Mount McKinley and then the massive Brooks Range, barrier between the flat plain of the Northern Slopes and the rest of Alaska. The last part of the flight was through dense cloud and it was a relief when the plane broke out of the fog with the runway already coming up.

For the uninitiated, Barrow comes as something of a shock. The climate is almost unbelievably harsh and the permafrost, lying just below the surface, is a major barrier to all forms of construction. Roads cannot be sealed and it is impossible to dig refuse pits. Nevertheless, I was quite unprepared for the plethora of derelict cars, broken machinery, abandoned snow buggies, bits of wood, metal, paper, plastic and garbage of all kinds which were scattered both

PREVIOUS PAGE
On guard. Female Snowy Owl in the low light of midnight.
OPPOSITE, TOP LEFT
Barrow, the most northerly town in North America and a very long way from anywhere
OPPOSITE, TOP RIGHT
Tundra in spring. The land begins to emerge from the snow.
OPPOSITE, BOTTOM
Snowy Owl sign - Barrow. The Inupiat revere the Snowy Owl yet still hunt it.

TOP
The beautiful Red Phalarope, probably the commonest bird on the tundra.
BOTTOM
Male Pectoral Sandpiper, newly arrived and already claiming a territory with the tundra still covered in snow."

throughout the town and for some distance beyond its borders. Kai Curry-Lindahl, the great Swedish biologist, once wrote of the degraded splendour of the lands around the Mediterranean as "Eden in a Ruined Landscape". Barrow has not yet reached that state but, set amid the pristine beauty of the snow-covered tundra, the contrast was jarring.

However, I was there to look for Snowy Owls. The last contact with Denver Holt had been very heartening. He was not yet in Alaska but his researcher there, Julie Petersen, reported Snowy Owls "Everywhere" and had already found one nest. Within an hour of arriving, we were out in the field.

The land around Barrow is quite flat, its' shores facing north into the Arctic Ocean. The winter had been particularly severe and the sea was still frozen hard. Ashore, the tundra remained almost entirely snow-covered but, although it was cold, the thaw had begun. We headed for a small patch of snow-free tundra with a shallow melt lake beside it. There were ducks on the lake, long-tailed Oldsquaws, American Wigeon and a few elegant but shy Pintail. They are frequently shot at and are wary.

Released, at last, from its covering of snow, the tundra looked brown and lifeless but a closer approach revealed it to be vibrant with shorebirds, newly arrived from the south. They had little time to get through their nesting cycle and, already, the posturing and pairing had begun. These were birds that I knew only as the rather drab waders, which spend their winters around the estuaries and salt marshes of the more temperate parts of the world. Now they were there with their spectacular breeding colours and dramatic displays.

Tiny Semi-palmated Sandpipers rose in the air like larks, planing down to earth again with a strange buzzing noise, reminiscent of the sound made by a piece of cardboard against the spokes of a moving bicycle wheel. Pectoral Sandpipers strutted around in their finery, choosing patches of elevated ground to puff out their black-streaked breast feathers and then breaking off to chase other males from their newly selected territory.

In the little pools there were phalarope, mostly the vividly coloured Red Phalarope but also a few of the more subtly plumaged Red-necked. Almost alone among shorebirds, phalaropes prefer swimming to walking and their method of display is to sit on the water and spin like a top, seemingly endlessly. Often, male and female would spin together, side by side, and Alan came up with the theory that males always spun anti-clockwise and females clockwise. I watched them and sometimes it was true but I was never convinced.

The shorebirds were not the only new arrivals. Jaegers were staking out favourable pieces of higher ground for their nest sites. On this first day, they

were all Pomarine but, by the end of the week, we were also seeing both Arctic and the elegantly graceful Long-tailed Jaegers. Later, they would wreak havoc among the nesting shorebirds and probably with the Snowy Owls too. Our goal was also Snowy Owls and we set off on our search.

Snowbound tundra is a strange yet fascinating medium to work in. Flat, almost featureless and often fogbound, it is a place where distance and perspective very readily become distorted. I had expected that, just as in the Australian desert, distances would be foreshortened but found, in practice, that it was just the opposite with some features being two or three times as far away as I had estimated. At least dark objects showed up clearly in the snow but a white owl against a white background was not going to be easy to see.

Julie might have reported Snowy Owls "everywhere" but, for the first few hours, we saw no evidence of it. Then, far away, on a patch of slightly rising ground, I could just make out a small white mound, which stood out even from the untouched snow surrounding it. To the naked eye, it looked like some child's abandoned snowman but, through the glasses, it was revealed as our first Snowy Owl. At that distance, it was as featureless as the snow itself, save for the black points of the two eyes and bill. From the purity of its white plumage, it was almost certainly a male.

We moved a hundred metres closer and, only then, spotted the head of a second owl, much closer than the first one. It was sitting in a depression on top of a little snow-free knoll and seemed certain to be on a nest. This was a darker bird than the first one and, even as we watched, it stood, picked up a small animal in its bill and flew to the first owl, dropping the prey at its feet in the snow. If we had had any doubts about the sexes, these were now answered when the original owl at once mounted the bird from the nest, balancing with slowly waving wings in a copulation which lasted for nearly half a minute. When the male jumped down, the female at once returned to the nest, while he waited a moment and then flew to land beside her where he swallowed the prey.

This reversal of sex roles in the prey offering was interesting but I did not know enough about Snowies to say if it was unusual. With the female involved in incubation, it is most likely that the prey had been caught by the male, who may have hunted so effectively that the female had an oversupply lying beside her in the nest.

The following day, we saw copulation with this pair again. He was sitting some 300 metres from the nest and flew towards it for half the distance to come down again on the snow. As he landed, she left the nest to fly to him

and they mated at once. He brought no food and she was back on the nest so quickly that it had been left uncovered for less than a minute. In this icy environment, it does not take long for eggs to chill.

So far, we had not yet made contact with Julie Petersen and arranged to do so on the tundra the next morning. She arrived on a four-wheeled motor bike, seemingly impervious to the rigours of the climate. Her news was better than we could ever have expected. Including the new one, which we had found, she now had twenty one nests and was coming upon fresh ones every day. The protocol of her study kept her from going close to any of them at this stage but, from her distant observations, she concluded that none of them yet had young.

With Julie's help, we now had a wide choice of nests to study but, with limited time, I had to select one and stay with it. I chose one that was within easy access and sight of a road but where my blind, 400 metres off the road through the snow, was unlikely to attract the attention of the casual passer-by. The nest was on a small earthen hummock, the only piece of ground in the area which was clear of snow and I wondered if it would have still been snow-covered when the female started to lay, a week or more before. Despite her proximity to the road, the female was quite difficult to see against the snow and we experienced this with every one of the nests which we saw. It would be a different story after the thaw when they would stand out like beacons in the night.

Now came the task of accustoming the owl to the blind. I wanted to keep disturbance to a minimum and had no idea how she would react to my presence. Some ground-nesting birds appear to realise the vulnerability of their situation and are very prone to desert. We assembled the blind at a distance and walked in through the snow. We were 200 metres away when she flew and we set the blind down at once, pegging it firmly against the wind. Long before we reached the road, she was back on the nest.

That evening, we moved the blind to within 100 metres and, the next morning, to 70. It would take one more move before it was close enough for photography but the most pleasing feature was that the owl treated our presence almost with indifference, sailing back to land directly on the nest, sometimes when we had hardly begun our walk back to the road. By contrast, the male, who had ignored us up to now, began to see us as invaders in his territory. Much of his time was spent guarding his nest from the top of one of the tundra's lines of electricity poles and, from there, he gave a deep double hoot, a signal to his mate that there was danger around. For the time being, that was his only reaction but it was a foretaste of actions to come.

While we waited to spend time in the blind, there was much to see. There had been frost in the early morning, enough to put sparklets of rime on the tundra grasses and a thin film of ice on the puddles but it was soon gone and the thaw was progressing apace. In two days, the melt pools had doubled in size and, where there had been unbroken tracts of snow, the land was now dotted with the brown of the emerging tundra. Ducks and shorebirds were spreading out into these new areas. Tundra Swans and White-fronted Geese had arrived, already paired and looking to start nesting at once. There were Golden Plover, resplendent in the black and gold of their breeding plumage and a pair of Pacific Loons came in on one of the melt ponds, now almost large enough to be called a lake.

Now we too were beginning to see Snowy Owls everywhere. The males were particularly fond of using electricity poles as watch towers, giving them a far greater field of view than the low hummocks and snowdrifts, which formed the only natural elevations. We saw three more nests, all on little hummocks of rock or soil. Clearly these were among the first places to become clear of snow and were above the level which could become inundated in the thaw. However, they also helped to make the sitting owl very conspicuous and may have increased the risk of predation.

I walked in on three of the nests to see what stage they had reached. It was June 9th and almost certainly too early yet for any of them to have young. At the nest where we had watched the pair copulating, there were four eggs and this clutch may not have been complete. Of the other two, one held five eggs and the other eight; big, creamy white ovoids, which, as with all owls, were completely without markings. There was no nest material but all lay in distinct cup-shaped depressions in the ground and were surrounded by a scattering of owl feathers and animal fur.

As we walked in, the females watched us, making no attempt at concealment but flying when we were still some distance away. There appeared to be an appreciable age difference between these females with one having fine dark bars and chevrons on the breast and upper wings, the signs of a young bird, while another and presumably older one was almost pure white.

So rich was the life of the tundra that every new walk seemed to produce something new and it was while checking the Snowy Owl nests that we started to see Short-eared Owls. They too were going to take advantage of the abundance of lemmings but probably needed the ground cover to thicken before they began to nest. Interestingly, the only lemmings which we saw were already in the bills and talons of owls and jaegers but signs of them were everywhere with tunnels beneath the snow and burrows going into some of the little hillocks where the ground was softest. Clearly they had been active long before the thaw started.

By the third day, we had worked the blind to within thirty metres of our Snowy Owl nest and I was ready to have my first session. With three people to see me in, I felt confident that the female would not realise that I was still there but there is always that feeling of anxiety when first starting with a new bird.

I need not have worried. She left the nest reluctantly, going no more than two hundred metres, where she landed on the snow, watching. Alan and Margaret had hardly started to walk away before she halved her distance from the nest and, long before they had reached the road, she was back on, gliding in low above the ground to rise and stall against the breeze, dropping straight onto the nest. She settled at once onto the eggs, stretching her head and neck up several times as she made herself comfortable.

Now I had my first chance to admire her at reasonably close quarters. Here was a bird which, as well as being exquisitely beautiful, was also superbly designed for its frigid environment. The shape was all curves, the contours of a Russian doll, with no angles or prominences to catch the wind and lose heat. Amid this, the details of the face were obscured, with the feathers of the large disc fluffed out around the eyes while the bill was almost buried in a ruff of comb-like feathers. Only when the owl yawned was the true size of the bill and gape evident. The eyes too were heavily protected against the cold and, when she closed them, the thickly feathered lower lids came up like two warm muffs. When she stood up, I could see the protective coverings of her legs and feet, densely feathered right to the toes.

This was a fully mature female and there was little in her plumage that was not white. There were a few blackish marks on her forehead, some black flecks on the wings and a finely barred upper tail but that was all. From the little that I had seen of her mate, he was even whiter. There was little activity during that first session and she had not moved when Alan came to relieve me four hours later. We moved the blind again, placing it now only twenty metres from the nest.

Now I wanted to spend every possible moment in the hide and we were back the next morning, dodging the melt pools and ploughing through deep snow, which had water running beneath it. The male hooted as we approached but the female was now quite accustomed to us and was back on the nest even faster than before. We were in a latitude of perpetual daylight but, despite this, there was fog with flat, grey lighting and a white horizon which was going to make photography difficult.

PREVIOUS PAGE
Tundra Swans, the commonest large waterfowl of the Barrow tundra.
OPPOSITE, TOP
At the 1999 nest, the female looks out over snow-covered tundra
OPPOSITE, BOTTOM
Snowy Owl nest. In good years, clutches of eight are quite common.

Four White-fronted Geese arrived, firmly separated into pairs, each couple seemingly intent on claiming a patch of tundra near the Snowy Owl nest and not wanting the company of the others. Each gander tried to drive the other away, half flying, half running with outstretched neck and snapping bill. It is well known that geese try to site their nests near Snowy Owls, apparently deriving some protection from predators in doing this. It is protection that may be short lived for there are records of the newly hatched goslings ending up as food for young Snowy Owls.

Late in the morning, a Raven flew behind the blind, calling. It sounded as though it was mobbing something and then, from the same direction, came a single owl hoot. Two minutes later, the female stood up and left the nest, flying away to the east. I lost sight of her but, after a very short interval, she returned, flying in with a lemming in her bill. I tried to follow her with the camera and, for the first time, she baulked at the sight of the lens, veering away to land on the snow. She stared at the blind, gave a quiet, grating scream, swallowed the lemming and flew to the nest. In six sessions in the blind over three days, that was the only prey that the male brought but it would be a different story once there were young in the nest.

When I started that session, the blind was surrounded by snow with a pencil-wide strip in front of me just starting to melt. Within four hours, that strip had become a metre-wide stream and I was sitting with my feet in icy water trying to find raised spots to keep my equipment dry. It was time to move the blind again to slightly higher ground.

My last session in the blind was uneventful, late in the evening but, at last, with good light. When I had finished, I walked the final few metres for my first look at the nest. There were five eggs but I had hardly taken this in when there was a single warning hoot and I looked up to see the male Snowy Owl less than ten metres away and diving straight at me with all the ferocity of an attacking goshawk. I ducked violently and he cleaved through the air where my head had just been, bill snapping like a set of castanets. He did not return but it was a salutary warning ever to be on the alert.

The next morning, I came back to remove the blind, watchful for any signs of aggression on the part of the owl. He circled me as I approached and my eyes never left him. Some birds of prey will only attack from behind but I felt that this owl would come at me from any angle. I was right and, as I neared the nest, he began his stoop, gathering speed and aiming straight at my head. I stood my ground, watching him grow bigger in the viewfinder as I tried to photograph his dive. I waited for as long as I dared, then pressed the shutter and threw

OPPOSITE
Attacking Snowy Owl. The 1999 male was very aggressive around the nest.

myself to the ground all in one movement as he whistled past, raking talons almost parting my hair. It was an exhilarating experience and he repeated it twice more before deciding that I could not be driven off and landing in the snow.

I picked up the blind and walked away, saddened that I had to leave so soon yet glowing from the experiences that I had had with this dramatic and singular owl.

With my fieldwork over, I had time for reflection and to study Julie's breeding maps. They showed a remarkable density of nests, particularly as all of them had been found in less than three weeks, certainly leaving more undiscovered. In an area of about sixty square miles, there were nineteen known nests. These were by no means evenly spread and, with the local map divided by a one mile grid, there was one square with three nests and two more with two. I did not visit any of these so cannot say whether there was any interaction between the pairs. At the nest where I had my blind, there were two further nests within less than a mile, one to the east and one to the south and I never saw birds from these nests anywhere near mine.

The ability of this barren-looking environment to sustain such richness of life is a source of total wonder. Owls, jaegers, swans, geese, ducks, loons and shorebirds jostle for space, most of them travelling for great distances to come and raise their young here. I have seen the phenomenon of the Australian

desert coming to life after rains but even that was not on the scale of the bursting of life that was taking place here.

Sadly, I had to leave even before the first owl's egg hatched but Julie was still there and kept me informed about her research. By the end of the season, she had found 29 Snowy Owl nests, which held an average of five eggs. Predictably, in this harsh climate, there was a high failure rate and only 14 succeeded in fledging young. Julie was uncertain of the causes of failure but with Arctic Foxes, jaegers, cold and starvation there were plenty of barriers to successful breeding.

Of the successful pairs, the number of young fledged averaged somewhere between two and three but there was considerable variation. The owls which I considered to be "My pair" were the most successful of all, laying five eggs and raising five owlets to fly. They were also the most aggressive birds and perhaps there is a link here. The extent of their aggression was vividly described by Julie in her e-mails to me. Not only did the male attack her but he was joined by the female, a most unusual occurrence. So belligerent were these attacks that, on her last visit to band the chicks, she was forced to cover the last fifty yards crawling on her stomach while the male stooped and struck her repeatedly, tearing his talons across her protective backpack as he raced through. For the experienced Julie, it was an exhilarating performance but there was danger in it too and one false move could easily have resulted in serious injury.

Dangerous or not, I was envious that I was not there to go through the experience. I had come to the Arctic for two weeks but, if I had come for the whole summer, it would still not have been enough. I resolved that, one day, I would return to renew my love affair with the Snowy Owls.

For the next four years, I followed the fortunes of the Snowy Owls. In 2000, surprisingly, they again bred in numbers but I had no chance to return. Then, as expected, 2001 and 2002 were both poor seasons with hardly any lemmings, few owls and no nests. The lemmings rarely have three bad years in a row so, for 2003, I had high expectations.

That year, the snows melted late. I was in regular contact with Robert Suydam but May passed and then the first half of June and he was still unsure about the owls. With airline flights almost fully booked, I took a gamble and decided to go. Margaret and I flew in on July 7th., over four weeks later than in 1999. Fortunately, Denver had arrived there too and he played a big part in our success.

The tundra in June and the tundra in July are very different places. In June, it is a land of snow and ice with just tiny patches of brown land and open water, concentrating the ducks and shorebirds into the only little areas that

OPPOSITE
On the tundra. Young male
Snowy Owl watching for
lemmings.

they can use. In July, the snow and ice have all gone, running off into a profusion of shallow lakes, leaving most of the land as dry ground. At first, it seemed that most of the birds had gone too, but this was an illusion. Now, with vast areas available, they had dispersed, staking out their territories and making their nests in the close vegetation. It took only a short walk to start flushing small shorebirds from their nests, many of them already with tiny, downy chicks. Ducks were nesting on the tundra too and, at the edge of one small lake, were the nests of two species of diver, loons in the local parlance, a pair of Pacific Loons and 200 metres away, a pair of Red-throated Loons. Their nests were so conspicuous that it seemed inconceivable that they could avoid the attentions of predators but they had survived so far. Only the jaegers seemed to have dropped off in numbers and this may have been significant for, like the Snowy Owls, they depend heavily on lemmings.

I went to see Denver, meeting him for the first time after years of exchanging e-mails. His news was not quite as good as I had hoped. It was no more than a moderate lemming year, resulting in only six pairs of Snowy Owls attempting to breed, three of which had already failed. Of the remaining three nests, one had a very shy female, while at the other two, little more than a kilometre apart, two females shared the same bigamous male. With lemmings scarce, there was obviously a concern that he might not be able to supply both nests, one of which, situated beside a motor bike track at the edge of a quarry, was so vulnerable that it seemed a minor miracle that the female had persisted. She had been pelted with stones by children and survived countless disturbances by motor bikes but had hatched at least three of her eight eggs with the oldest chick now 19 days old. There was also the risk from hunting, for the Inupiat still take Snowy Owls for food and feathers, a practice which continues, even though the bird is protected by law and is highly respected in Inupiat culture, where it is their local emblem. Denver had a blind nearby, not so much for photography, for it was out of sight of the nest, but as a deterrent to the motor bikes, causing them to take a small detour away from the site. Despite its' unfavourable situation, I decided to spend some time there.

As I walked in, with the nest still hidden behind a bluff, the male flew past, pure white and elegant. He had just delivered prey and I rounded the corner to see one of the chicks choking down a whole lemming. The female was nowhere to be seen but, within ten minutes, she was back at the nest, heralding her arrival with harsh screams and landing with a lemming in her bill. I could just see the head of one of the chicks as it seized the prey, not attempting to dismember it as it gulped it down whole.

OPPOSITE
Lining up for the stoop.
Female Snowy Owl about to
attack.

That was two lemmings in 20 minutes but it was not long before the female was demanding more. She screamed repeatedly, a shrill cry which degenerated into a wheeze and ended in a querulous croak. Within minutes, the male was there. He dropped down into the nest, deposited the lemming and was gone, barely having time to furl his wings. It was time enough for a chick to seize the lemming and, in moments, that was gone too. I never saw the male at either nest again.

I stayed for another two hours but there was no more activity. After a while, the female left. Denver had noticed her hunting for some days and, with an outside temperature of 10°C, the chicks were quite able to maintain their own body heat. At a little over three weeks of age, young Snowies start to wander from the nest, and the biggest two were already close to this, moving slowly and awkwardly as they stood up to take two tottering steps before collapsing again, necessitating an unsteady rise to the feet before attempting the next move. By the end of the week, they would be wandering 50 metres away.

For me, the second nest was an altogether better prospect, out on the open tundra where the ground sloped gently and my blind could look down into the nest. On July 8th., we went in with Denver's assistant Matt Seidensticker, walking across a tundra carpeted with flowers; pink Lousewort, white flowers of several species and the beautiful golden Arctic Poppy. We paused briefly to look in the nest, where there were three eggs and three chicks, soon to be joined by a fourth for one egg was chipped and about to hatch. The oldest chick was already 11 days old, giving it a huge advantage over the later ones if food supplies became short.

That evening, I went in the blind at 9.0pm. Far to the north of the Arctic Circle, we were in the zone of perpetual daylight where the sun does not set for 84 days, a wonderful season when there is very little incentive to go to bed at all. Its' offset comes in winter when the sun fails to rise for the same period, a situation which I would find very hard to endure.

We were still 600 metres away when the female flew. We hurried the rest of the way, I got quickly in the blind, Margaret left and, within two minutes, the owl was back, gliding up against the breeze to lose all forward motion and drop lightly onto the nest, surely as beautiful a sight as anything in nature.

In 1999, most days had been grey and misty but now the light was brilliant, the low sun picking out every detail of bird and surroundings. From the outset, she appeared completely relaxed and, in minutes, was asleep. A Golden Plover piped from a nearby mound, a Semi-palmated Sandpiper rose and fell with its' tremulous song-flight and there was not another sound.

OPPOSITE
Snowy Owl arriving at nest with Lemming
FOLLOWING PAGE
Female at nest amid arctic flowers, July 2003.

After an hour, the owl began rummaging in the bottom of the nest. She spent some time raking and deepening the cavity with her bill and then picked up a Brown Lemming which had been lying on the rim. She seemed about to eat it but then flew, taking it with her and landing a short distance away where she worried it but made no attempt to eat. Then she picked it up and flew back onto the nest.

At once, she started to feed the chicks, not the biggest one as I had expected, but the two small ones, snipping off tiny pieces and presenting them with great gentleness in the manner of hawks and eagles. All the while, she propped herself on the bends of her wings, a posture which I was to see repeatedly. Then she settled to brood.

I stayed there until after midnight, all the time in most beautiful light. I expected the male to come, for the chicks were still too small for the female to hunt herself, but he did not appear. Unlike his wife at the other nest, she made little protest about this, only occasionally giving a soft scream which, to me, was identical to the food begging call of a Black-shouldered Kite.

The next day, I had two more sessions in the blind. With 24 hours of daylight, opportunities for photography were almost limitless. Again the male did not come but I knew that the chicks were being fed. Two English friends had also used the blind and had seen the male bring in a Lapland Longspur and an unidentified wader, while the female had produced another wader from the bottom of the nest. Then, while walking nearby, they had seen the male carrying a Pintail. It seemed that I had simply been there at the wrong time. Nevertheless, it was probably an indication of lemming scarcity that the owls were taking so many birds. Denver has a vast amount of prey data over many years which has shown that 97% of prey consists of lemmings. This nest clearly had a much lower proportion than that.

On July 11th., I was in the blind when Matt arrived with two helpers to inspect the young and, if they were large enough, to band them. Usually, when disturbed, the female landed a short distance away and remained silent but now, seeing people at the nest, she barked loudly and my mind went back to the Ural Owls in Finland. Moments later, she was in the air, rising as she flew towards Matt before plummeting down to strike him a tearing blow on his crouching back. She rose and turned, her eyes never leaving the intruders and then the second stoop came from a different direction to end with another shuddering blow to Matt's back. With a bird weighing nearly three kilograms, the force of the strikes was immense and the potential for serious injury great. It was as well that there were several pairs of eyes to watch the bird as Matt concentrated on his job with the young.

There were still four chicks but now only one egg, a loss of two from the original seven eggs. There was great disparity between the sizes of the two biggest and two smallest chicks and, almost certainly, the little ones would not survive, a situation which occurs more often than not with ground nesting owls and also with harriers. Even the two largest young were still too small to band so Matt confined himself to weighing them, all the time under constant bombardment from the female owl who continued to stoop and strike, hitting him a total of 17 times, tearing a series of great rents in his almost new parka.

The night before we left, the smallest of the young owls in the quarry nest disappeared. We were never totally sure of its' fate but, some time after midnight, my English friends saw a car arrive there and a person walk to the nest. One of the many hazards which the owls face in Barrow is that of the young being taken for pets, a practice which rarely ends well for the owl. It seems almost certain that this is what happened. Fortunately, like Eagle Owls, young Snowy Owls start wandering as soon as they can walk and the bigger two had already left the nest and escaped detection.

Denver was concerned to check for himself and, on my last day, I went back with him. We were still half a kilometre away when he spotted that something was wrong. Near the nest was a four wheel motor bike and at least six people, one of whom appeared to have a gun. We assumed the worst and Denver leaped from the car as we drove up to confront the intruders. He was away for some time and, when he returned, was accompanied by six attentive young Inupiat boys, one of them carrying a long pole, which we had mistakenly thought to be a gun. They had found the young owls and had been harassing them but were not quite prepared to pick them up, fearful of their beaks and talons and the attentions of the protective female.

Denver was superb. He could have berated them but chose to talk to them about the birds; where they came from, what they lived on, the hazards that they faced in raising their young, their rarity and the fact that they were so special that here was a man, indicating me, who had come all the way from Australia to see them. The boys clustered around him as he showed them the safe and gentle way to pick up the young and then got two of them to go with him, each carrying a baby owl to a safer and more secluded spot. By the time he finished, he had produced six friends of the Snowy Owl who would try to ensure that the young were left in peace to fledge. It could so easily have ended in angry discord and how much better to teach the young the wonders of this bird and show them that the Snowy Owl is not just another animal to be shot and eaten. I was sad to leave but could not have finished on a better note. I had been fortunate beyond all expectations, amazingly privileged to have been able to spend time with this rare and fascinating bird.

Only later did I learn just how fortunate I had been. Our English friends stayed on for another two days but under very different circumstances. We had scarcely flown out of Barrow when a blizzard erupted, making conditions impossible for photography and very difficult even for removing the blind. The owls suffered too and the two smallest chicks at my nest died and disappeared. Hopefully, they were not totally wasted for, with the adults unable to hunt, they probably became food for their older siblings, a gruesome but necessary part of nature. However, there was nothing natural or necessary about the subsequent shooting of both adults at the quarry nest, the female fatally and the male probably so. Denver saw the male flying with a broken leg and then found the corpse of the female, shot and thrown on the tundra to rot. It seems that there will need to be a lot more education before the owls are safe from their human neighbours.

Now I am writing this on the very last day in July. In two days time in Barrow, the sun will set for the first time in twelve weeks, a very brief disappearance for it will dip below the horizon for just a moment at midnight. From then on, however, the days will shorten at breakneck speed, a quarter of an hour every day until, in the second week in November, the sun will cease to appear at all and will remain set until the first week in February. That will herald a season of bitter cold and perpetual night with only the midday twilight to soften the darkness. Few creatures can survive in these conditions but somehow, amazingly, the adult Snowy Owls do. For the young owls, only recently independent, it is too severe and many of them move south to appear in southern Canada and the northern states of USA. Not so the adults, most of which stay in the arctic, somehow finding food when nearly all other birds have gone and their favourite lemmings are hidden beneath the snow. Only the Arctic Hares and a few ducks remain and these must surely be difficult prey in the darkness of the long night. How the owls survive is a question that I cannot answer but it only adds to the respect and wonder that I feel for this bird, surely one of the most fascinating of all owls?

OPPOSITE
Snowy Owl chick, just at the wandering stage.

Argentina

Burrowing Owl

In the 1990's, my son Richard was living in Argentina. His work frequently took him out in the country and he often saw owls sitting on the ground beside the road. His first reaction was that they must have survived a hit from a car but he began to see so many that it seemed there must be another explanation. He rang me in Australia and we decided that they must be Burrowing Owls. Fortunately, I had plans to go and visit him there and would have a chance to see for myself.

Burrowing Owls! The archetypal ground-dwelling owls of the prairies, the deserts, the pampas and the other great grasslands of the Americas. I had long read about them and pictured them in my mind, at home in the treeless space of those vast plains.

How far off the mark was my mental image! When I found them, they were living among vacant lots of building land in a Buenos Aires housing estate. It bore scant resemblance to their traditional habitat. However, the surroundings in no way changed the appearance or the behaviour of the birds, intriguing little characters who would appeal even to those who profess a complete disinterest in natural history.

Buenos Aires, capital of Argentina, is a giant among cities, a huge metropolis of 11 million people, herded into a man-made environment of concrete, glass and bitumen. A 64 lane avenue carries the traffic in and out of the city centre and, if there is any sound of birds, it is drowned by the roar of the motor car.

A little further out, the houses do have gardens but crime is rife here, high fences are almost obligatory and there are guard dogs behind every one, ready to rush out and attack any creature that moves. It is not a place for a ground-dwelling owl.

Not everybody is happy with this way of life and there are some who look for a less constrained existence with more space and no threat of crime. Out of this desire have grown the "Barrios Privados", large, open housing estates with no fences between the houses, no guard dogs and no security alarms. There are golf courses, playing fields and recreation areas and it is only around the perimeter that there is an almost impregnable fence with the only entry past the armed sentries at the guard-house; the 21st century equivalent of the mediaeval walled city. Seen through Australian eyes, it seems a strange way to live but it suits many Argentinians and it also suits the Burrowing Owls which clearly are completely at home here.

We arrived at the gate, my host, Gustavo Ranowsky, showed his pass and we were through. I am not sure what I expected. I knew that there was a golf course there and had somehow pictured the owls in some secluded corner of the rough, away from the fairways and the traffic of players. Possibly they were there but that was not where we were heading. We drove along a curving suburban street, lined with new houses, well-kept gardens and neatly manicured lawns. This was a new barrio, still with vacant blocks of land and soon we came to the first of these, a quarter hectare square of rough-mown grass between the houses.

Just off the footpath was a hole like a rabbit burrow and, in its entrance, stood a dumpy little brown owl. Its feathers were fluffed out in composure and its lower legs and body were hidden in the hole, accentuating its squat appearance. Beside it, but standing outside the hole, was its mate, more alert, as it sensed that here were people who were not going to drive past but who had an interest in it. With its whole body in view, I could see now that this was a very long-legged owl and, with its head and neck stretched upwards, its bearing became erect and slim, in sharp contrast to that of its mate.

These birds were used to people and, when I cautiously got out of the car and assembled the camera, they stayed put, eyes never leaving me. They are diurnal owls and their brilliant yellow eyes bore this out, small and so well protected by the frowning eyebrows that the sun rarely shone into them. Apart from the posture, they were a very similar looking pair but the bird in the entrance was perceptibly darker and I took it to be the female.

I moved a little closer and this finally brought a move. The female withdrew down the burrow and, left alone, the male clearly felt vulnerable. Then he was in the air, his flight quick, round-winged and bouncing, a carbon copy of the flight of the Little Owl of Europe. This was his territory and he went only fifty metres, landing to turn and face me. He bobbed, a quick up and down, watching me all the time. It is a highly typical Burrowing Owl movement, so human in character that some Americans know it as the "How-de-do Owl". As well as being a sign of nervousness it appears that it is also a threat display but I was a bit too big for it to be effective. He tried it several times but, with no success, changed his tactic.

Now he stretched up to his full height, his bearing reminding me of the Prairie Dog and the African Meerkat. For a creature of the flat plains, every millimetre of extra height is an advantage and may be life saving. He wanted me to leave and told me so, calling with a sharp, goshawk-like "Kik-kik-kik-kik". With each "Kik" he puffed out his throat feathers, showing their white undersides in threat display. I had no wish to cause undue disturbance and moved on.

During that day I saw three more pieces of vacant land with Burrowing Owls and, on my next visit, two more. Gustavo assured me that this was only a very small proportion of the total living around the 250 hectare barrio and it was clear that there was a very significant population of owls there. Whether they had preceded or followed the barrio, nobody seemed to know. Whatever the answer, it seemed that many of them were going to have a short tenure there for I saw no completed houses with owls in their gardens. However, the golf course and other open areas would remain as suitable habitat and the owls' long-term future there was probably secure, even if the numbers were likely to fall.

I wondered how such a small area could sustain that concentration of birds. Much of their diet is insects and, in the cold winters of the Argentinian plain, these must become hard to find. They also take many small mammals but, in a modern suburban setting, it is hard to envisage that there will be so many of these that it will sustain a pair of owls to every few hectares. Interestingly, I saw no pellets around any of the six burrows which I visited.

It was only a few hundred metres to the next "owl estate" and here there were four birds close to the burrow, presumably an adult pair and two grown young. It was September and, I assumed, close to the start of the breeding season but, if my supposition was correct and these were young birds from the previous year, they still seemed very attached to their parents.

This group was not quite as approachable as the first pair and scattered, some landing back on the ground a short distance away while two perched on the roof of a new house. I was busy photographing these when a security guard appeared riding a bicycle. He carried an ancient shotgun but I surmised that it still worked and he looked worried. Fortunately, Gustavo was still with me and, after a lengthy discussion in Spanish, the guard finally got on his bicycle and left, shaking his head. I asked Gustavo what had transpired and he told me that the guard had thought that we must be taking photographs of the house for the tax department. When Gustavo told him that I was photographing the owls, he looked at him in disbelief, muttered "Strange" and went on his way.

At my next visit, ten days later, Gustavo could not come and I was on my own. With my Spanish being close to non-existent, he provided me with a letter of explanation to be produced during times of emergency. It was just as well, for I spent ten minutes in the hands of a highly suspicious guard who, even with the letter, was clearly inclined to throw me off the premises. It seems that bird watching is yet to catch on in Argentina.

PREVIOUS PAGE
Burrowing Owl pair at the entrance to their nest burrow.
OPPOSITE
Burrowing Owl on top of concrete pole. The owls were happy to use any elevated perches, natural or man-made.

At one owl site, a man was mowing the grass and the owls sat on a roof-top while he worked. He seemed quite unaware of the burrow, mowing right over the entrance to the hole but it was of no concern to the owls, which were back there within minutes of his leaving.

I measured the depth of two burrows. One went in for 60 centimetres and the other for a full metre, with both going down at an angle of about 30 degrees. In more natural areas, Burrowing Owls frequently take over the old holes of ground squirrels, prairie dogs and badgers but here, with none of these mammals present, it seemed likely that the owls had dug the burrows themselves. The entrances were heavily trampled and scattered with feathers and droppings but, strangely, no pellets. Perhaps they are deposited elsewhere for even a disintegrated insect pellet should have left some residue.

I left without having a chance for a night session with the owls. It was probably as well. Even with a letter of explanation, my presence in the darkness, hiding in a tent and firing off flashes, would have been a severe test for the credulity of the security guards.

TOP
The ever alert Burrowing Owl
BOTTOM
Burrowing Owl on roof-top. It was while I was photographing this bird that I was challenged by an armed guard who had decided that I was photo-graphing the house for the Argentinian Tax Department.

Austria

Eagle Owl

Long-Eared Owl

She sat on a rock, high against the cliff, motionless; a huge owl but dwarfed by the immensity of her surroundings. The Eagle Owl is a giant among owls, striking in appearance and a formidable hunter. The overall colour is a deep, rich brown with dramatic eyes, which may be vivid yellow, orange or, in some birds, a glowing brick red.

From four hundred metres away, I had little chance to appreciate her size or beauty and very little time either. For half a minute she stayed and was then gone, dropping off the ledge and flying directly away with broad wings and powerful beats.

Mediaeval people knew this owl well, for it plundered their chickens and game but they made use of it too, tethering a captive one to a post so as to attract and trap the inevitable gathering of mobbing birds.

In many ways, little has changed today for it is still shot by hunters and farmers and, in parts of its range, live birds are still used as a lure. To survive at all, it has had to live by its wits. Small wonder that it is shy.

This was a bird that I had long wanted to see and, to find it, I came to Austria and to Hans Frey, a legend among Eagle Owl men. During a twenty year study, he has found over two hundred Eagle Owl breeding territories throughout eastern Austria and has banded well over a thousand young. He is also the mastermind behind an ambitious project to re-introduce the Lammergeyer to the European Alps and a major breeding station is situated in his own garden.

A veterinarian by profession, he also runs a considerable rehabilitation programme for sick and injured birds of prey and, as if that is not enough, does research and teaching at the Veterinary University in Vienna. I came to Hans in the middle of May 1996, staying with him at the Lammergeyer breeding station just outside Vienna.

My arrival there was a revelation in itself. The station is at the last house in the village street and, from outside, looks just like any of the other houses. Appearances can be deceptive. As we passed through the garden gate, kestrels took off in all directions, some of the many wild birds which breed there in both natural sites and nest boxes.

Inside, the two hectare garden was almost filled with spacious aviaries, the smaller ones occupied by raptors in various stages of recovery from sickness or injury; Common Buzzards, Black Kites, a Hobby, a Saker, numerous kestrels, Barn Owls, Tawny Owls, Long-eared and Short-eared Owls and even a solitary Eagle Owl. Some of them had injuries, which would keep them permanently in captivity but many of these were breeding and their young would be able to go back to the wild.

OPPOSITE
Looking out from his daytime roost – the magnificent European Eagle Owl.

These were the small cages but most of the space was taken up by a series of large flight aviaries housing the Lammergeyers. There were over thirty adults, mostly in pairs and many of them with young in the nest. I had seen Lammergeyers in the wild but always in flight and at a great distance. Now, to be so close to these great birds was a memorable experience. Later, I would go to the Alps with Hans for the annual release of the young but, today, I could only admire these superb birds.

An alternative name for the Lammergeyer is Bearded Vulture but I feel it is a misnomer. These birds were not in the least vulturine with fully feathered necks and heads, bright red eyes and the extraordinary beard, a long tuft of black feathers which runs through the eye, across the bill and then projects below it in a bristling brush.

Evening came and there were more surprises. As I sat in the house, from above my head came the snoring and hissing of Barn Owls, which were breeding wild in the roof. Their voices were joined by a chorus of Little Owls, also breeding wild in nest boxes against the house. Then a Tawny Owl left its roost and added its sharp cries and I thought that I had never before sat through such a cacophony of owl sounds.

In two days time, Hans was due to begin his annual Eagle Owl grand tour, checking the occupancy of breeding sites and banding young. This would continue for several weeks but, until then, I was to go with Fred Söllner, another Eagle Owl expert and wildlife photographer. Fred's English was about as bad as my German but we managed to establish a remarkable understanding and, in two days, became good friends, a friendship which was to grow over the ensuing years.

Not only did Fred know of many Eagle Owls in the wild. He had also built a cliff in his own garden, complete with overhanging ledges, a cave and a pair of breeding Eagle Owls, all housed within a huge aviary. This natural appearance was to prove a godsend when, later, I found it almost impossible to approach within range of birds in the field.

At Heudürr, above the Danube, I saw my first wild Eagle Owl. It was a superb setting. The valley of the Danube here is quite narrow and the wide river, muddied by melting snows, runs swiftly. Ancient villages cling to its banks, each village dominated by the church spire above the red roofs. On the south side the hills rise gradually but the north side of the valley is steep and rocky with cliffs, which, in places, come close to the river bank.

We left the car along a muddy track beside a vineyard and started to climb. The hillside is terraced for vines, each succeeding terrace narrower because of

TOP
Fred Söllner going over the cliff to an Eagle Owl nest.
BOTTOM
Eagle Owl's view. The outlook along the Danube from the Heudürr nest.

PREVIOUS PAGE
Eagle Owl. The chicks at
Nussdorf. *Photo Fred Söllner*
TOP
Wöllersdorf. Two Hedgehog
skins on the cliff-top, visiting
sign of an Eagle Owl and the
clue to finding the nest.
BOTTOM
Hans Frey takes an Eagle Owl
chick from the Wöllersdorf
nest for banding.

the steepness. The higher slopes were once under vines too but these have long been left to revert to hill pasture.

We climbed on, through grassland carpeted with spring flowers of many colours. All the time, the Danube lay below us, lifeline of the region for centuries. The river traffic was constant; huge barges, often pushing two or three more like water trains, luxury passenger ships, small boats, naval patrols. Moving downstream, they glided past swiftly and smoothly but it was a different story the other way as they pushed up big bow waves, moving slowly against the power of the current.

High above the river, we worked our way around the opening of a valley, which ran back from the water. The far slope was wooded but, on our side, it was steep with cliffs and rocky outcrops.

We looked up the valley into a broken cliff face with clefts, crags and narrow, grassy ledges, searching for the Eagle Owl. It was Fred who spotted her, sitting upright at the entrance to a shady cleft. It took me some time to find her, the mottled rufous plumage seeming to become almost part of the cliff. Quite still with ear tufts erect, she gave the impression of being unconcerned but then, without warning, flew, even though we were some distance away. I was to find this the norm with Eagle Owls. In Austria they are shot at regularly and are correspondingly wary.

Thirty metres on from her look-out, and at a slightly lower level, was the nest, sited, typically, beneath an overhanging rock. The grass was flattened over a length of some three metres and, at one end, were the two owlets. Still covered in butterscotch coloured down, they were about five weeks old, already with well formed flight feathers beneath the down.

The approach to the nest looked difficult but Fred had been there before. We scrambled down the hillside, made a five metre descent by rope and then wriggled along a narrow ledge to the nest.

It was worth it. The view from the ledge was superb; the busy river, the villages, still hazy with morning smoke, the grape vines, just showing the first shoots of the new season and, above them, the forests in all the lushness of the new spring.

The floor of the nest was strewn with prey debris. Eagle Owls are immensely powerful hunters and few wild creatures are safe from them. This pair was taking mainly birds and there were piles of kestrel and crow feathers with smaller numbers from gulls. There was mammal fur too and I was surprised to see pieces of Hedgehog skin, complete with spines. This armoured animal is immune to the attacks of most predators but it seems that the Eagle Owl has its measure and I was to find Hedgehog remains at almost every nest site that I visited.

The two young were together against the back of the chamber, orange eyes glaring defiantly. We admired them, photographed them, banded them and left, heaving ourselves back up the rope and across the slopes, passing through a patch of glorious blue irises as we took a different route down.

In ten days, first with Fred and then with Hans, I visited twenty three Eagle Owl territories, barely a tenth of the total known to Hans but, nevertheless, more than the total of nests known throughout Austria only a few years ago.

In these territories, we found fifteen active nests, all with one or two young, which ranged in age from about three to nearly six weeks. It was late May and the young would normally have been further advanced but the winter of 1995-96 had been a very hard one, delaying the start of breeding for an average of about three weeks.

In some parts of its range, the Eagle Owl nests in trees, using the old nests of other large birds but this is rare in Austria where the vast majority of nests are on the ground. All but one of the breeding sites were on natural cliffs or in quarries, with a roughly equal balance between stone and sand quarries. One pair only usually nested at the foot of trees but, in drenching rain, we were unable to find any sign of it.

For Hans, the timing of his visit to each nest was crucial. Before about four weeks of age, the young are too small to band but, between five and six weeks, they become mobile and tend to wander away from the nest. Sometimes this makes them impossible to find and, in Finland, I have seen a six-week old Eagle Owl which had moved nearly four hundred metres from the nest. On cliffs, there is also the risk that the disturbance may lead to them falling, possibly to their deaths. With the majority of broods all being at the same stage of development, the banding season is a time of frenetic activity for Hans, who usually manages to band over sixty young owls each year.

Interestingly, although the birds are so shy, they seem to sense when human presence is a threat and when the people are concerned with other things. Our arrival anywhere within sight of the guardian adult invariably caused it to fly but Fred knew of an instance where an active nest was within five metres of men working in a quarry. So secretive are the owls that the men had never noticed the nest and the birds clearly did not feel themselves to be threatened.

Some of the nests were very easy to find, situated at a traditional spot or in an area where there were only one or two possible sites to choose. Others were found only after a long search or some ornithological detective work.

Wöllersdorf was one of these; a steep natural cliff with a long base, which had for years been the home of Eagle Owls. With Hans, I walked up through

OPPOSITE
The Wöllersdorf chicks, just under four weeks old."

moist, green beech forest with the cliff hidden from view until we were almost through the fringing zone of pines.

The signs were not good. Two of the most frequently used sites were empty and two rock climbers, roped together, were in mid-ascent of the cliff. We walked along the base of the cliff, looking for telltale signs of the owls. There were none but we found plenty of signs of climbers with steel rings and pitons hammered into the rock all over the cliff face. The Wöllersdorf cliff had become a popular spot.

Then, along the top of the cliff, we came upon two Hedgehog skins, lying together and turned inside out. Only an Eagle Owl leaves a visiting card like this. Further along the cliff were the scattered feathers of a Common Buzzard and then, back at the base of the cliff, some whitewash. There was an Eagle Owl nest somewhere nearby. We looked up and the female flew from the pine tree where she had been all the time, watching both us and her nest.

Now it did not take long to find it, half way up the cliff and under the almost obligatory overhang. There were two owlets, less than four weeks old and smaller than any that we had yet seen. Around them was the usual scatter of food remains and we identified the feathers of Jay and Common Partridge, species which we had not previously recorded as prey.

Eagle Owls like to know who is around in their breeding territory and the view from this nest was commanding, up and down a green valley and over the tops of the trees to the distant villages. Most of the sites were even more open than this and, with the shy and unapproachable nature of the birds, it seemed that I had no chance of putting a hide close enough to a nest to be able to watch and photograph at night.

Then we came to Gumpoldskirchen, an ancient village south of Vienna, famous for its wine. There is a huge stone quarry here, horseshoe shaped with its vertical walls a hundred metres high in some places. Here was a nest that Hans had known for years and, looking across the quarry, I could make out the dark opening of a small cleft in the rock with the even darker shape of the adult owl, backed into the deep shade of the cave. From that distance, she looked tiny.

One shoulder of the horseshoe lay quite close to the cave. Silver Birch scrub grew right to the top of the cliff, a possible site for a hide, level with the nest and with an oblique view into the entrance. It was worth the climb to have a look and I found myself twenty five metres from the nest with an unobstructed view and a hidden approach to the hide. It was a long way to throw a flash but I had almost given up hope of finding a workable nest. The scrub was so dense that I was able to fashion a cocoon of a hide at the cliff edge without

OPPOSITE, TOP
The cliff at Gumpoldskirchen, 100 metres high. The nest hole is arrowed and the hide site circled.
OPPOSITE, BOTTOM
In fading light, the female Eagle Owl arrives at the nest on the high cliff of Gumpoldskirchen.

using any cloth at all. With only one night left in Austria, there was no time to spare. I would spend the whole of that night in the hide.

It was not a comfortable session. The hide was tiny and, by the time I had found room for the camera and tripod, I was left sitting on an upturned box, my back against a tree and with almost nowhere to put my legs. The flashes were outside, concealed in the grass; too well concealed it transpired, for some unnoticed grass stems in front of them gave a greenish tinge to the photographs. At that distance, I had no option but to use very fast film.

Hans left me, making himself as conspicuous as possible. The female was nowhere to be seen but, inevitably, the young had spotted us and sat in the cave entrance, craning their necks to get a better look. This behaviour would not have been lost on their mother and it was as well for Hans to make a very public departure. I settled down through the slow passage of the European twilight.

At nine o'clock, the sun had been set for half an hour and the young were becoming active. They were much bigger than any of the other owlets we had seen, probably more than six weeks old, fully feathered and very close to flying. Side by side, they stood in the cave entrance, leaning forward and flapping their wings vigorously. Only a toe-hold separated them from an eighty metre fall and I feared that they would go.

Half an hour later, the male began to call from the far side of the quarry, a soft, musical "Oohoo-ooo", the first "Oo" almost inaudible, the "Hoo" rising up the scale and then slurring into a descending "Ooo". The German for Eagle Owl is "Uhu", a wonderfully onomatopoeic name which fits the bird perfectly. The whole call lasted barely a second and I found it remarkably soft for a bird of such size. He went on for a full fifteen minutes, calling several times a minute but without any reply that I could hear from the female.

By now it was ten o'clock but the quarry was lit by a high moon. From far below came the almost constant roar of trains on the main line to Vienna but the quarry was a different world and it was silent and still. Then she came to the nest! I heard a single, short scream and there was still just enough light for me to make out her dark form as she flew in. I did not dare to show a torch and, with the owl lost in the blackness of the nest cave, had no idea what she was doing. I fired the flash, expecting her to flee at once but there was no reaction. I fired again and only then did the shadowed wings drop away from the cliff face.

For several minutes there was silence. Then a harsh, cackling scream rang echoing across the quarry. A few seconds later it came again and then again, continuing four or five times a minute without pause. Even with the knowledge of its source, it was a spine-chilling sound, disturbingly eerie and

OPPOSITE
First day of freedom.
A Gumpoldskirchen chick on the morning after climbing from the nest.

menacing. My Finnish friends call it "The Devil's Laughter" and it is an aptly fitting description. Clearly it was an alarm call, the equivalent of the shivering bleating of a disturbed Australian Powerful Owl. For half an hour it continued until, very slowly, the intensity began to subside and then, finally, it ceased.

Half an hour later she came to the nest again. By now, the moon had almost gone but I could just make out her approaching shape. Already she seemed to have accepted the flash as a natural phenomenon and stayed while I took several shots.

I think that was her last visit. At one o'clock the male began calling again and was eventually answered by a single scream but, if she did come to the nest, I was not aware of it.

Summer nights in Europe are short. By four o'clock, there was a suggestion of light on the horizon while the first songbirds had begun their chorus some time before. As the light strengthened, the owlets launched into some particularly energetic wing flapping, leaning forward as they practiced for their first flight. A fall seemed inevitable and then it came as the larger one leaned a little too far, tipped forward and went over the edge. Miraculously, it managed to grab onto a narrow ledge as it fell and there it stayed, a metre below the nest, safe, but with the prospect of a long wait, for it had little chance of being able to clamber back.

As with many owls, the female was active at dawn too, screaming and approaching so close to the nest that I thought she would come in but the enthusiasm slowly waned and daylight came with her perched on the cliff a hundred metres away. With my appearance from the hide she flew, pursued at once by a pair of Ravens but she had met them many times before and, when she landed on the cliff across the quarry, they left her. I felt sure that she was there for the day.

That ended my time with the Eagle Owls and there remained only the trip to the Alps to release the young Lammergeyers. It was a long drive and a tight fit in a tiny Renault with two passengers, a large dog, a pile of equipment and the two young Lammergeyers, comfortably bedded down in a man-made nest of sheep's wool which took up most of the back of the vehicle. In the previous ten years, over sixty young birds had been released in the mountains and the population was now well- established although successful breeding had yet to take place.

Our destination was a small hut at the end of a muddy track, high up in a remote alpine valley. I had expected the release to be an equally remote affair but arrived to find that this was a considerable social and media event. There were two film crews there plus Bavarian Television and a host of sponsors, conservationists and raptor enthusiasts. That night, the little hut was filled to capacity and the air buzzed with enthusiastic talk, mostly in German but with

OPPOSITE
Lammergeyer. One of Hans Frey's captive breeding birds.

snatches too of English and Italian for this was an international gathering.

There was snow in the night and, in the morning, the release site, a cave on the mountainside, was only just below the snow line. It was a five hundred metre climb carrying cameras, tripods and the precious boxes with the Lammergeyers. Once in the cave, they were on their own and would not see their parents again, nor the people who, hidden from them, would drop food into the cave. They were still a month short of flying and would be given food three times a week, not only until they could fly but until they had become completely independent and had ceased to return to the cave to find the food. As we opened the boxes, they shuffled straight into the cave as though this had been their home from birth.

The next morning, we left in mist and sleety rain that was almost snow, walking out of the valley as the road had been blocked by a rock fall. High on a cliff, at the edge of the mist, were three Griffon Vultures and, on the next ledge, two adult Lammergeyers. If Hans ever wondered whether his project was worthwhile, surely this gave him the answer.

I had expected that this would be the end of my Eagle Owl work but, back home in Australia, I could not get them out of my mind. Surely it should be possible to find a pair where I could work a hide appreciably closer than at Gumpoldskirchen?

In May 2000 I tried again. Hans Frey had already found an active nest in the Burgenland, south of Vienna and I was to have unstinting help and hospitality from Fred Söllner and his family.

Fred and his wife Irene met me at Vienna airport and we went straight to find Hans' nest. It was in a small quarry and, although neither Fred nor I had been there before, the site under a rock overhang was obvious. With a clear view into it from across the quarry, this would have been an excellent site for me. It was empty! Three weeks before, the female had been incubating but, now, the only sign of Eagle Owls was a single primary feather. There was nothing to indicate what had befallen them but the Eagle Owls two biggest enemies here are foxes and jaegers.

Jaegers, the Austrian name for hunters, have a huge influence on predators in Austria. Their quarry is mainly deer, hare and pheasants and their wooden shooting hides, raised on stilts, are scattered far and wide throughout the woods and farmland. No threat to their game is tolerated, be it real or merely perceived, and any bird with a hooked beak is destroyed without mercy. Kestrels, Buzzards and Long-eared Owls all suffer but it is the Eagle Owl which is seen as the arch enemy. Unfortunately, with its predilection for using traditional nest sites, it is an easy target for the hunters. Over the next few days, Fred and I were to realise just how easy.

The next day, we went to Nussdorf. Here there is an extensive area of wooded hillside with a number of rocky outcrops and three old nest sites. I had seen young here in 1996.

On the way in, Fred was uneasy. He is an astute observer and noticed a few broken twigs and branches, almost certainly caused by human presence. None of the nest sites was occupied and then, a short distance from the last one, we found the rotted corpse of an adult Eagle Owl. It was generally intact but the right wing was shattered. This was not the work of a scavenger on an already dead bird. Only a shot would have caused this.

Two days later, we climbed the cliff above S't Michel on the Danube. Here was a long-used Eagle Owl site but there were no owls. Instead, there were a few feathers and two spent cartridge cases on the floor of the old nest. There was no doubt about what had happened here.

The same day, we returned to Heudürr where, four years before, I had been

delighted by the two young owls and the spectacular view down the river. This time we went to the other side of the narrow valley to be able to look across and into the nest.

We were not the only ones to have this idea. Arriving at the spot with the best view to the other side, we noticed that this had been opened up by some extensive and recent pruning of the hillside oak trees. The far cliff was liberally coated with whitewash but the nest, occupied only two weeks before, was empty. We looked more closely at the pruning and realised that it had been done to give a direct line of sight for a shot into the nest. Later, we found the male owl but he was alone and there seemed little doubt what had befallen his mate. This was an easy nest to spot from across the valley, made more so by all the whitewash and it was almost inevitable that the hunters would eventually find it.

We did find two other occupied nests during the week but both were so well hidden and inaccessible that photography was out of the question.

In the end, I returned to Gumpoldskirchen. At least the hunters had not found this one and there were again two young. This time, Fred and I spent three nights there together in conditions that were as uncomfortable as before, taking it in turns to keep watch from the hide while the other tried to sleep among the rocks, wedged against a tree to avoid rolling down the 45° slope. The photography too was just as difficult. Both adults were almost completely silent and the female's visits all came without any warning so that there were times when I was unsure if she was at the nest or not. Once or twice, I watched her great round-winged shadow sweeping up to the cliff in the moonlight but there were just as many times when I missed her completely.

The young were further advanced than in 1996 and at least I was there to see the first one leave the nest and gradually work its way up the hillside. It had cleared life's first hurdle but there would be many more to come, for the world of an Austrian Eagle Owl is one of unrelenting hazard.

I returned to Australia while Fred stayed in touch and told me of the progress of his beloved Eagle Owls. The news was not good. Gumpoldskirchen had been successful but the other two nests, inaccessible though they were, were not safe from the depredations of the jaegers. At both nests, one of the adults was shot, the other abandoned the site and the young were left to starve. Out of Fred's seven active nests at the start of the season, six had failed. In every one, the evidence pointed towards the jaegers as the cause.

It is a wretched situation and Fred is fighting an almost lone battle to give the owls protection. It is a huge task. The jaeger is part of an almost sacred Austrian tradition and to challenge his ways is akin to sacrilege. It will need more than Fred alone to end the slaughter but, without this, the Eagle Owls of Austria face a very uncertain future.

My story was, I thought, ended but now, in 2002, I can add two heartening postscripts.

In 1997, for the first time in 100 years, a wild-bred Lammergeyer chick flew from its nest in the French Alps, offspring of two captive-bred parents, which had been released over eight years before. In the following two seasons, this pair twice more fledged a chick while, in 1998, a second pair, in the Swiss Alps, was also successful. It will take many more successes before the new Lammergeyer population can begin to look safe but it is a triumph for Hans Frey and his co-workers in many parts of Europe.

With the Eagle Owls, Fred Söllner has also had a notable victory. Alone and against all advice, he took on the entrenched power of the jaegers in court. It was a huge risk, which could have resulted in financial ruin but he won his case with costs and there is now a ruling protecting the Eagle Owls from molestation by the hunters. With no mechanism for enforcement, it now remains to be seen if the hunters will respect the judgment. The battle is not yet won but it is an excellent start, an illustration of what can be achieved by one determined individual.

OPPOSITE
Diversion from Eagle Owls – a young Long-eared Owl which we found during our travels.
FOLLOWING PAGE
A rare moment with both birds at the nest, the male in full view.
Photo Fred Söllner

Christmas Island

Christmas Island Hawk Owl

There are only two ways to go to Christmas Island; by commercial aircraft or by sailing your own boat. The former is quick, comfortable and relatively inexpensive; the latter slow, rough and decidedly costly. Margaret and I chose the aircraft.

Christmas Island is a very lonely island in the Indian Ocean. Lying 10° south of the equator, it is 300Km south of Java, 1400 Km from the coast of Western Australia and a very long way from anywhere else. It is also a very small island, barely 20 kilometres long and only half that in width, a tiny piece of land in the great emptiness of the ocean.

People never settled there and it was uninhabited until Britain took possession in 1888. Land birds have also found either the passage difficult or the environment hostile and only eleven species have been able to establish themselves there naturally. Three of these, the White-breasted Waterhen, White-faced Heron and Nankeen Kestrel are new arrivals, their success made possible through the new habitats created by phosphate mining.

Among the remainder are six endemics, five full species and one sub-species, indicative of long occupation of the island and very infrequent new arrivals. One of these endemics is the Christmas Island Hawk Owl, the reason for our visit.

Christmas Island is a unique island in many ways. The top of an extinct volcano, it spent aeons beneath the ocean, acquiring a deep covering of organic phosphate, before it rose from the water 50 million years ago when it was approximately 1000Km south of its present position.

Until British settlement, it was totally covered in rain forest, dense and lush with trees up to 50 metres high on the sheltered, western side. Its shores are rocky and inhospitable with vertical cliffs, jagged boulders and reefs of coarse limestone, which can tear open a boat at a touch. Only the seabirds find landing easy and, for them, there is a plethora of ledges and caves for resting and breeding.

For mariners, there is only Flying Fish Cove, a partly sheltered inlet with a shingly beach, easy to approach now with the long, steel jetty but a different story for the early voyagers, trying to make land through a litter of limestone boulders.

There were two small yachts at anchor in the cove and, on our first evening, we went to the island's tavern where we found both their crews. They had both courage and determination. A Scotsman and his daughter had just finished the first leg of the voyage from Australia back to Europe. From there, they were heading west, past Sri Lanka, into the Red Sea and then Suez. They had heard about the pirates who roam the Red Sea almost unchallenged and were a little concerned. I felt that they had good cause.

An Australian doctor and his wife had left civilisation behind and were circling the world. Their route would take them further south to Cocos Island, then Madagascar and on to Africa. Their steering was by tiller and, with no self-steering or radar, they kept two hour watches throughout every night, an exhausting task with only the two of them to do it.

Richard Hill had, like us, come the easy way. He was engaged in a two year study of the hawk owl and was the key to our success in finding it. He did not let us down.

Christmas Island is a place of strange contrasts. Lying in the path of the south-east trades, it is swept constantly by them, a speck of land in a turbulent ocean; too small to have any calming effect on the wind.

Any visitor to the island will first notice the seabirds. They breed there in their thousands, some of them widespread and familiar species but some found nowhere else in the world; Abbott's Booby with its long, slender wings, the Christmas Island Frigatebird and the beautiful Golden Bosunbird, a race of the White-tailed Tropicbird, which has the usual white replaced by glowing gold.

Human settlement is rarely all bad for wildlife and here it is the frigatebirds which have recognised the source of fresh water at the resort swimming pool, the only fresh water on the island outside the forest. All day, a cloud of them circulates above the pool, each one manoeuvring itself downwind before making its raking approach, skimming low to the surface and dropping its lower mandible vertically to scoop up a beakful of water in passing. Most have perfected the art but there are many tentative young birds which abort their approach short of their target while a few others come in too low, hit the water and are left to struggle ignominiously to the side with flight feathers waterlogged. There is no buoyancy in a frigate bird's plumage and any bird which did this at sea would almost certainly die.

Around the coastline, the seabirds are in their element. All day they stream along the cliffs, stiff-winged, slipping across the face of the rising air. Masters of gliding flight, they are at home where the wind blows strongest; frigatebirds, boobies, noddies, bosunbirds; all birds of the ocean but needing the land for breeding.

Ten metres back from the cliff top is a different world. This is the edge of the rainforest and, once inside, the sea might be a thousand kilometres away. It is a place of stillness and twilight, sealed off from the world of wind and spray by the dense forest canopy. On the forest floor, it is as though the air never moves. There are scents of wet leaves, rotting logs and fungus while the scuttering footsteps of the land crabs carry clearly across the ground. Only from above is there still the sound of wind hissing across the canopy in a reminder that this is indeed an oceanic island.

OPPOSITE, TOP
Christmas Island Coast.
OPPOSITE, BOTTOM
Christmas Island Frigatebird.
An endless stream of them drank in flight from the resort swimming pool."

Only six species of bird have managed to establish themselves in this forest. Interestingly, two of them are raptors, one goshawk and one owl. This is the home of the Christmas Island Hawk Owl.

Until recently, the Christmas Island Hawk Owl was as little known as almost any owl in the world. Nobody was sure if it was a full species or, if only a sub-species, what was its parent stock. The nest had never been found, there was no information on food or size of territory and even the estimate of population was little better than a guess. This was the task which confronted Richard Hill and he had two years to try to answer as many of these questions as possible. By the time that we arrived there, we were able to benefit from his efforts over nearly eighteen months.

On Christmas Island, the hawk owl is neither rare nor shy but, nevertheless, the finding of the first bird was a considerable challenge. The forest is dense, the trees vary from big to huge and there was almost no prior knowledge to work from. Later, with taped calls, radio-tagged birds and some observations, it all became a bit easier but Richard had to start as a pioneer.

We join him on a circuit of his owl roosting sites. His research has shown that there is a pair of owls to about every fifteen hectares but this is virgin rainforest and they are not easy to find.

We start on the plateau, the highest part of the island, where there are few crabs to sweep the forest floor and the vegetation is thickest, a tangle of vines, pandanus and fallen trees. It is machete country and Richard has already cut a track, linking the roost sites of several pairs. The owls tend to roost low, often in the cover of the pandanus and this, coupled with their complete lack of fear, has made them not too difficult for Richard to catch. There are complicated methods of catching owls, working at night with decoy birds, mist nets and taped calls but, to his surprise, Richard has found that the best way with these birds is to approach them slowly with a noose on the end of a pole, rather as the ancient wildfowlers used to take seabirds on the cliffs of the Scottish islands. In this way, he has been able to catch and radio-tag a number of birds, one of which then led him to its nest, the very first Christmas Island Hawk Owl nest ever to be found.

This time, we are not so lucky. Richard takes us to site after site, many of them no higher than eye level, but there is no sign of an owl. On this island of high rainfall, the telltale whitewash does not last for long but even Richard's pellet catching nets below habitual perches contain only leaves. He shows us the site of last year's nest, a hollowed broken limb, high up in a Syzigium, one of the biggest trees in the forest. Probably it would have been used again this year but another branch has fallen and blocked the entrance. Once we come across a great circle of spattered whitewash but there are groaning calls coming from high above it and we can just see a young Abbott's Booby in its treetop nest. It will spend a year there before becoming independent of its parents.

We move to another area of the forest, lower down where the crabs clean the forest floor and eat off the seedlings as soon as they push through the ground. Crabs dominate the Christmas Island environment and, with their catholic appetites and predatory habits, may well be the reason for the paucity of bird and animal species on the island. By far the commonest are the Red Land Crabs, not unlike the ones we had seen in Costa Rica but bigger. The forest floor is pitted with their holes for this is their home for almost the entire year. Only in November do they move and then the entire population makes the journey down to the sea to mate and spawn. With 120 million crabs making the journey at once, this is an incredible sight, a moving red carpet covering every inch of the island's lower slopes, usually in the last quarter of the November moon. It is not a good time to be out driving for it is impossible to avoid them and the claws of a large crab can pierce a car tyre as readily as a steel nail.

The lower forest may be better for walking but the owls are no easier to find and a circuit of several more known roosts is again unsuccessful. Prospects are looking distinctly poor when we come to a group of pandanus palms giving ample cover and many perches. Here, sitting close together, are two small red owls. Their breasts are closely barred like the Rufous Owl of Australia but they are even redder and only a fraction of the size, smaller than the Australian Boobook and lacking that bird's frowning eyebrows. They are asleep and, even though we are only a few metres away, show no sign of letting us wake them. Richard had expected them to be nesting but this is clearly not the case.

This may be the only time that I see them and I take a few photographs and settle down to wait for dusk. The owls sleep on, totally unconcerned by my presence.

Night comes early to the rainforest and, well before sunset, the light starts to fade. I watch the owls begin to stir, stretching a wing, then a leg, then a wing on the other side. When one stands up high on the perch and shakes itself I know that they will soon fly and that I will probably see no more of them. It comes then as a complete surprise when the first one planes down from the roost and lands on a low branch less than a metre above my head. Before I have overcome the shock, the second owl follows it, gliding down for the two to sit side by side where they remain for several minutes.

OPPOSITE, TOP
Roosting in deep shade – first sight of the Christmas Island Hawk Owl.
OPPOSITE, BOTTOM LEFT
Christmas Island is famous for its' vast population of the endemic Christmas Island Red Crab. Its' similarity to the red land crabs of Costa Rica is striking.
OPPOSITE, BOTTOM RIGHT
The Robber Crab that invaded my open camera case.

Now all signs of sleep have gone. The brilliant yellow eyes are open wide and the birds are fully alert although still quite relaxed. As yet, I am uncertain of the sexes. One bird is slightly paler with neater plumage and closer barring on breast and tail. It seems the more active of the two and, even though it is slightly smaller, I take it to be the male, an assumption which, I later realise, is wrong.

For five minutes I revel in the proximity of these glorious little owls and then they are gone, disappearing into the blackness of the forest night. When I turn round I have a visitor, a Robber Crab.

The Robber Crab is the world's biggest land crustacean and Christmas Island is one of its strongholds. Big Robbers may be several kilos in weight and their claws are immensely powerful. Although primarily vegetarian, they will eat almost anything and even totally inedible objects are worth a try. During a recent army training exercise, one sleeping soldier awoke to find that the Robbers had removed not only his boots but also his rifle.

My Robber is straddled across the top of my open camera box, attempting to remove the contents. So far it has not had time to succeed and the tough Nikon cameras and lenses are probably crab proof anyway. However, there are also electric wires and cable releases and the crab could snip these like a pair of secateurs. I send him on his way and take more care from then on. Robber Crabs have learned that people mean food, particularly at night when the crabs are most active.

I thought that I had probably seen the last of the hawk owls but, to my surprise, the roost was occupied for the next four nights, once by a single bird but otherwise by the pair. It was as well, for these were the only owls that we saw during our whole stay.

Every night we learned something new. Usually the awakening process was accompanied by a little calling, recognizably similar to the pair-bonding "Porr porr porr" of the Boobook but higher, harsher and delivered very sotto voce. Only once, after leaving the roost, did one bird break into a typical *Ninox* double call, in a voice which had the exact metre of a Boobook but was pitched higher and with a barking rather than a hooting character.

On the fourth night, both birds flew and then returned to the roosting perch, where they spent ten minutes mutually grooming each other. This looked suspiciously like a prelude to breeding and this was confirmed on the following night when they flew down to a perch almost beside me, sidled up to each other and mated, confirming that it was the larger and darker bird which was the male. The next moment they flew, one leading the other through the forest. Darkness soon swallowed them but not before I could see

OPPOSITE
The Christmas Island Hawk Owl flew down to perch level with my head on a Pandanus Palm.
FOLLOWING PAGE
Watching Margaret's every move – two Christmas Island Hawk Owls.

that they had set a course straight towards a tree which Richard had suspected as a possible nest site. I did not see them again but it seemed certain that breeding was about to start.

Two nights afterwards, Richard came across another pair with a very recently fledged chick. These must have started nesting at least three months before, evidence of a very protracted season. It was then early August.

Three days later, we left the island with many questions still unanswered. High on this was the owl's identity. Was it a sub-species or had the time come to recognise it as a species in its own right? If it was only a sub-species, the next question was "Of what"? Three years later, those answers would come but, in 1995, when I was there, they were still the subject of much debate and conjecture.

Van Tets, in 1967, regarded the bird as a sub-species of the Oriental Hawk Owl, *Ninox scutulata*. With a distribution throughout South-east Asia, Borneo and Sumatra, this is geographically the closest *Ninox* to Christmas Island. However, its appearance is appreciably different from the Christmas Island Hawk Owl which, in more recent years, was thought likely to be a sub-species of the Moluccan Hawk Owl, *N. squamipila*. This theory had its problems too as there is a gap of about 2,500 kilometres between Christmas Island and the nearest Moluccan Hawk Owls, a gap which takes in Java and a host of other islands where the owl does not occur. I am not a taxonomist but, from everything that I had seen and read, I was strongly inclined to the view that the Christmas Island Hawk Owl was a full species. With the advent of DNA molecular testing, it seemed possible that the question could be settled beyond doubt.

That answer came in 1998 through the work of Norman, Christidis, Westerman and Hill. They carried out exhaustive tests, not only on the Christmas Island Hawk Owl and on *N. squamipila* but also on several races of the Boobook, *N. novaeseelandiae*, and on the Barking Owl, *N.connivens*, Rufous Owl, *N.rufa*, and Powerful Owl, *N.strenua*. These provided conclusive proof that the Christmas Island Hawk Owl is, indeed, a full species which now takes the scientific name of *Ninox natalis*. With a total population of less than 1000 birds and a place to live of a little over 130 square kilometres this makes it one of the most rare and vulnerable owl species in the world.

I do not want to end on a technical note. My main memories of Christmas Island will be of its rugged beauty, its glorious climate, the richness of all its wildlife and the extraordinary confiding nature of almost all its birds.

On my last day there, a Christmas Island Goshawk came down a narrow forest track and nearly hit the windscreen of my car. Any mainland goshawk

PREVIOUS PAGE
Any doubts about gender were resolved when the hawk owls mated in front of me.
TOP & BOTTOM
Christmas Island Thrush and Goshawk, two of the island's endemic birds.

would have fled in fright but not a Christmas Island one. It swooped up into a tree above me and then dived down to catch what appeared to be a small crab, only metres from my feet. Then it flew into the forest but went scarcely past the first tree before perching and starting to eat, allowing me to inch closer and closer with camera and flash until I was standing almost beside it, taking pictures with a short-focus lens. As though that was not enough, it finished its meal and flew from the forest to land on the car's roof rack before departing. It seemed an appropriate farewell to everything I had enjoyed there.

This should be the idyllic finish to an equally idyllic story. With an end to phosphate mining and the declaration of a national park by the Australian Government it might be have been expected that no obstacles would stand in the way of Christmas Island and its wildlife. Life is not always like that, however, and nobody had foreseen the arrival of the Yellow Crazy Ant. This African invader was accidentally introduced to Christmas Island in the 1930's but took some years to establish itself in numbers and was not regarded as a problem. Only when the red crabs began to disappear from parts of the island and dieback started to affect areas of forest was it realised that crazy ants were anything but harmless.

They cause damage in a number of ways. They farm and nurture sap-sucking scale insects, allowing them to overwhelm the foliage of the forest canopy and cause dieback. They consume any animal matter in their path, eating insects, nestling birds and, most alarmingly, the red crabs. The red crabs are first blinded with formic acid squirted into their eyes and then, unable to feed or navigate, fall prey to the voracious hordes. This has decimated crab numbers in parts of the island and had a progressive effect too for it is the crabs which keep the forest floor clear of vegetation and their demise is quickly followed by the appearance of thickets of saplings, radically changing the habitat.

Christmas Island is not the only island invaded by the crazy ant. On the Seychelles they arrived on Bird Island in 1991 and have already spread across half the island, wreaking havoc among the nesting seabirds. Hopefully, this kind of disaster can be avoided on Christmas Island. At present, the crazy ants are confined to a fairly small proportion of the island and considerable efforts are being made to control and destroy them. It is a task fraught with problems but, if it fails, the outlook is grim for the unique life of this wonderful island.

Costa Rica

Spectacled Owl
Ferruginous Pygmy Owl
Pacific Screech Owl

If anybody wants to capture my interest, mention an owl. To me all owls are fascinating but there are a few whose appeal surpasses logic and become almost mystical. Among these is the Spectacled Owl, the strikingly unusual great owl of Central and South America. I had longed dreamed of seeing one and to turn dream to reality, I travelled to Costa Rica and sought the help of Agustin Zuniga.

Agustin is a passionate man. A plant biochemist by profession, he has a profound knowledge of the rainforest and a deep commitment to its preservation.

His perspective of the rainforest is a balance of science and fervour. He sees it as a place of peace and beauty. He sees it as an environment of great complexity and fragility, irreplaceable once lost. He sees it as home for a vast number of species beyond the trees themselves; plants, mammals, birds, reptiles, insects, many of them able to exist only in the rainforest. He sees it as a source of foods and fruits, unknown commercially yet highly palatable and nutritious. He has lived through the discovery of a host of forest substances; medicines, dyes, perfumes; and knows that a myriad more are waiting to be found. He has watched the wholesale destruction of the rainforest, much of it for a perceived gain which turns out to be no gain at all.

With his intricate knowledge of the forest, our chances of success are surely good. Margaret and I spend several days in his company and our association ranges far beyond the search for our elusive quarry.

We are at Tiskita on the Pacific coast in the far south-west of the country. Here the rainforest is almost virginal and appears endless but this is an illusion. Agustin tells me of the huge areas of forest destroyed for cattle ranching, using slash and burn techniques that produce a few years pasture from impoverished soils before the nutrients are exhausted and the ranchers moved on to treat the next piece of forest in the same way. He speaks of the banana plantations on the Caribbean coast, producing for a satiated market. As fruit prices have fallen, the plantations have grown even larger, creating an avian desert where few birds live and which is now so vast that it has blocked the altitudinal migration between coast and mountains which is crucial to the survival of many bird species.

These are some of the facts but there is no pessimism in Agustin's approach. He has an almost messianic view of his role in protecting and educating. He speaks of "My People", of teaching them to understand the forest; to use it without destroying it; to grow native fruits and crops instead of exotics; to treat the forest as a friend and not an enemy. He is an idealist but there is a practical side to his schemes. Would that there were more like him.

OPPOSITE
The Spectacled Owl burst from cover and flew down the creek. I thought it had gone but it flew only a short distance, allowing me to stalk slowly into camera range.

The search for the Spectacled Owl proves to be a classic owl quest, simultaneously fascinating and frustrating. The Spectacled Owl is the big forest owl of Central America, a bird of thick rainforest, given to roosting along creeks and in gullies. Knowing the Rufous Owl of Australia, this sounds somehow familiar. Despite the daunting terrain, there seems to be a chance of success.

There is also something very familiar about the forest itself. It is green and lush with huge trees of many species, arboreal ferns and orchids, great strangler figs and long ropes of twisted vines, which trail down from the treetops. Many trees have flowers or fruit but, in the dim light of the forest floor, the ground is almost bare.

Not everything is familiar. Crabs abound in this forest, small land crabs with brilliant red legs and undersides, set against two prominent yellow false eyes in the shiny black carapace. They cover the forest floor in thousands, sensing my approach from fifty metres away and scuttling for their burrows so that the air is filled with the rustling of their footsteps. Once a year, on a full moon, they move en masse to the edge of the sea to lay eggs but, at all other times, the forest is their home.

In the trees there are monkeys, little Squirrel Monkeys that move through the forest in whistling, chattering troupes of up to fifty animals. They seem to appear from nowhere, streaming through the trees as though travelling on a highway. Vulnerable to predators, their safety lies in staying close together and keeping on the move. Small babies travel on their mothers' backs while older young must keep up with the troupe. Their agility is amazing and I watch them racing effortlessly along the topside of a swaying electric cable, defying gravity in an eighty metre dash between its two anchor points.

Last year, the Spectacled Owls bred somewhere in this rainforest. No one found the nest but the parents brought their snowy-white fledgling to roost near the forest lodge and it stayed there for several weeks. Then, wraith-like, adults and young all disappeared. I talk to Peter Aspinall, owner of the lodge, who has seen an owl snatch a young monkey from its mother's back. I hear of how it catches land crabs on the forest floor. By now, the search for the Spectacled Owl has become something of a crusade.

It is a long, hot search. Most reported sightings seem to have been along the main creek where the bare branches reach out above the water, deeply shaded yet with room to move beneath them. There is an abundance of sites which fit this description.

On the sixth day, it is finally the owls which reveal themselves to me. In the deep, narrow gully I would probably have walked past them but they burst from

OPPOSITE, TOP
The Red Crab of Costa Rica.
At Tiskita, on the Pacific
Coast, the forest floor teemed
with them"
OPPOSITE, BOTTOM
Squirrel Monkeys at Tiskita;
agile and appealing but reported
to be a favourite prey of the
Spectacled Owl

cover simultaneously. One disappears from sight into the forest but the other stops and turns to face me, framed through a gap in the foliage. It is a big owl, chocolate brown in colour, paler on the breast and with the brilliant yellow eyes dramatically outlined by the white "spectacles". The plumage is different but the look, the size and the setting are all strikingly reminiscent of the Rufous Owl.

It watches and Margaret watches back while I creep away to fetch the camera. The tactic almost succeeds. In ten minutes I am back and the owl has not moved. Then, as I line up the long lens, it slowly turns, slips off its perch and is gone, lifting over a ridge and down into deep forest. We search for an hour but without success. Perhaps evening will reveal more.

5-30p.m. We are back, standing in a small clearing in the bed of the creek. The light is still bright but the sun is about to set and, at 5 degrees north, the night follows very quickly.

It is like a scene revisited. I have done it so many times before in Australia; the tall trees, the fading light, shapes becoming shadows, colours fading to silhouettes.

It may seem a familiar scene but there are differences. While there is still colour in the sky, the Swallow-tailed Kites come over, six of them, extraordinarily lithe and graceful, twisting and swooping in the still air in their hunt for insects. All other soaring raptors have left the sky but such is the buoyancy of these birds that they can stay aloft without so much as the flick of a wing tip.

6-0p.m. The first bats are moving and the pinpoint sparks of fireflies dance like spectres through the forest. The air is still but the sound of the distant ocean is constant, overpowering the frogs, the cicadas and the few last birds. Five minutes later, one of the owls gives its only call, a series of hooting pops, descending in pitch and volume but increasing in tempo, "Pop, oop, oop, oop, upupup". We wait, but there are no more calls and no sign of an owl. Then our torch fails and we make our way back along the narrow track in darkness. This is our last night at Tiskita and we will have to leave with only the first piece of the puzzle in place.

Hacienda Solimar! It lies on a coastal plain, separated from Tiskita by ranks of forested mountains and 400Km of rough road. Oscar Gonzalez Pacheco is the owner, a large and hospitable man with a booming voice, a thriving construction business, a prize-winning Brahman cattle stud and a love of birds. His three thousand acres have been developed with great understanding, leaving much pristine country and with the cattle nowhere threatening to overwhelm the environment. Strangely, his driving ambition seems to be to leave it all behind, climb onto a Harley Davidson motor bike and ride off into the sunset!

OPPOSITE, TOP
Turquoise-browed Motmot at entrance to its earthen burrow, one of the many colourful birds of Costa Rica.
OPPOSITE, BOTTOM
Swallow-tailed Kite. This elegant raptor frequently soared over the forests at Tiskita.

The hacienda is a joy to stay in. Its open verandahs look out onto a parkland of spreading Rain Trees and Giant Cassias while the tropical climate has removed the need for glass in the windows. Everywhere there is colour and movement. Iguanas are in profusion, some nearly two metres long and with a propensity to enter the house if a door is left open. Hummingbirds dart from flower to flower, tiny avian helicopters, able to place themselves in space with microscopic precision. Beside the hacienda is the nest hole of some Hoffmann's Woodpeckers', the young being fed by two females and one male. There are brilliant trogons, competing for nest holes with the woodpeckers, and colourful motmots, which somehow manoeuvre their long, racquet-shaped tails into earthen nest tunnels without breaking them.

"Come and see our plastic owl" says Oscar, leading me into the garden and to a massive Rain Tree. A small owl is perched close in to the trunk but it is

Two aspects of the Pacific Screech Owl:-
RIGHT
By day. Almost invisible with feathers drawn in tightly and eyes almost closed.
FAR RIGHT
After sunset. Feathers relaxed, eyes wide open and about to leave for the night's hunting.

certainly not plastic although, from its statuesque immobility, it could have passed as such. The Pacific Screech Owl is one of the scops owls, a group found in every continent in the world apart from Australasia and Antarctica. Masters of camouflage, they spend the day pressed motionless against the bark of their roost tree, invisible to all but the very keenest eyes. The long ear tufts are held erect, helping to break the shape of the head and it is only with darkness that these are gradually relaxed, the eyes begin to open and the piece of bark reveals itself as an owl.

I watch this bird on several evenings. The sun does not set until six o'clock when the light is still bright. Ten minutes later it is almost dark and, without warning. the owl is gone, springing high from its perch up through the tree and into the night. Not once do I see it again until dawn.

And so to the Spectacled Owl. Tiskita has been fascinating but less than

successful. Solimar is our last chance.

Our hope lies in our guide Demetrio. Young, cheerful and immensely helpful, he knows his Solimar birds backwards. He speaks no English and we have no Spanish but he has learned the English name of every bird in the Costa Rican field guide and this will prove to be a godsend. For the rest, we converse through the aid of a pocket Spanish dictionary with much gesticulation and laughter. It is slow and, at times, farcical but we gain a remarkable understanding of each other.

Transport is either on foot or with Emilio, a rotund and jovial farmer. His spluttering, rattling pick-up has seen many better days but it appears to be the only vehicle in the district. Starting it is a recurrent problem and the treadless tyres produce almost no traction at all but, somehow, Emilio always manages to get through. The cab has room only for Margaret as passenger, so Demetrio and I sit on the tail gate, a precarious and bone-jarring perch but one which gives an excellent all round view.

Solimar country is a patchwork of lush pasture and residual woodland, intersected by rainforest creeks, lagoons and rivers. All the local people are connected with the estate and their simple wooden houses are scattered about the property; earth-floored, without electricity and with pigs and chickens running both outside and in. It is a peasant's existence but all seem immensely happy and friendly.

There are owls in the open country. A Barn Owl roosts habitually high above the ground in the fronds of a tall palm. Safe from all predators, it seems strangely nervous there and flies at our approach, at once attracting the attention of a horde of big magpie-jays, which mob it mercilessly, threatening to buffet it to the ground.

Soft, repeated pipings prove to come from a pair of Ferruginous Pygmy Owls, tiny day-flying owls, which are little bigger than the finches and warblers, which they prey on. They too excite fury among the neighbouring birds and their every move is accompanied by a chattering mob of small passerines. They are well accustomed to it and take no notice at all.

We come round a corner to find a milling mob of vultures, crowded round a desiccated cow carcass. It has long been reduced to mere bones and leather but, for a vulture, there must be some residual food value.

There is a sense of expectancy as we walk into the first rainforest creek. Huge trees arch over the channel to blot out the sun but the way along the water is quite open. Horizontal branches abound beneath deep shade and it looks ideal for a roosting owl.

There is no hope of secrecy here. Howler Monkeys have seen us coming and

OPPOSITE, TOP
Demetrio, our guide at Solimar. His help was crucial to finding the Spectacled Owl
OPPOSITE, BOTTOM
A Ferruginous Pygmy Owl in the grounds of Hacienda Solimar. Like other pygmy owls, this diurnal owl is often accompanied by a noisy collection of mobbing small birds

shout their alarms, blood-curdling bayings that sound more like wolfhound than monkey. I am fearful lest they panic the owl before we even get close.

Moments later, we come round a bend in the creek and the big, dark owl explodes from its refuge. I expect it to go right away but it flies into a dense thicket and stops. Looking intently through the glasses, I can just see a bright yellow eye watching us through a tangle of twigs and leaves.

Big owls rarely perch unless they have an open escape route and so it proves with this one. Moving slowly and cautiously, we work ourselves round to a point where we have a clear view into where it is perched and we revel in the sight of this dramatically striking owl.

It is still a long way off and, after its initial behaviour, I hardly dare hope that it will allow me within photographic range. There is only one way to find out. Gradually I work my way forward, first into distant range and then closer and closer, taking pictures as I go, until the bird is almost filling the photographic frame. The eyes never leave me but the owl seems quite relaxed and even shuts one eye as though close to sleep. It is, of course, a deception and, as I look down to change films, it leaves, slipping silently from its perch and away into the forest.

Three days later, in a different creek but similar circumstances, we see a second owl. Again it breaks from cover and then stops to look back at us, seemingly at ease once it has a choice of flight paths.

Perhaps this reluctance to leave is an indication of a nest site nearby. There is very little known of the Spectacled Owl's breeding and Demetrio is unable to enlighten us. I look in vain for the big termite-made tree hollows which abound in Australia. There are plenty of small holes left by woodpeckers and trogons but a Spectacled Owl needs something much larger than this. They must exist somewhere but, looking from the ground, it is impossible to search thoroughly.

Our last session with the Spectacled Owls is at night. Along the creek, it is quickly inky dark and the only hope of finding the owl is if it calls. There are bats, fireflies and the Common Pauraque, the nightjar of the Central American forests, but no Spectacled Owl. All the sounds come from frogs, cicadas and a single Black and White Owl, whose musical hooting comes frustratingly close without our ever catching a glimpse of it.

OPPOSITE
Spectacled Owl under the rainforest canopy; a dramatically striking owl

Finland

Ural Owl
European Pygmy Owl
Tengmalm's Owl
Great Grey Owl

RIGHT
Pertti Saurola prepares to
climb to an owl nest box.

FINLAND! What sort of a country will this be? The land of Spruce Forests, Saunas and Sibelius! A land of deep snow, icy winds and the midnight sun! A land of rugged, romantic and fiercely patriotic people! A land where the owls must survive the rigours of a near Arctic winter, yet be able to hunt when the summer days are perpetually light.

These are some of my thoughts and questions as the plane begins its descent into Helsinki. In my ignorance, I suspect I am being both vague and fanciful. In some ways I am but much of it is remarkably close to the truth.

Our host, Pertti Saurola, certainly fits into my mental image. A tall man with wild hair and a forest of beard, he is the very picture of the proud Norseman, an epithet which is undoubtedly correct. He is also, however, a scholar, a writer and one of the finest baritones in Finland. On the ornithological side, he is head of bird ringing at the Helsinki Museum and one of the world's great experts on owls. He has climbed to more owl nests probably than any other person on this planet and, when not involved with owls, has done the same thing at countless Osprey nests, an even more testing and hazardous task. On both of these subjects, Finnish owls and Ospreys, he has written fascinating and authoritative books. Away from birds, he is a member of Kamariherrat, a distinguished choir of eight unaccompanied male voices which has sung in many parts of the world and made a number of CDs; a redoubtable man. Over the years, he will become one of our greatest friends but this, in 1994, is our first real meeting.

From Helsinki, we head north to our home for the next week, a little wooden house in the forest, dark but full of character, smelling of wood smoke and leather. The setting is idyllic, off the road, with a narrow footpath as the only means of approach to the lake just below, only recently free of winter ice. In this rustic atmosphere, modern services would have seemed out of place and there is no electricity or running water. The breeze soughs softly through the spruces but there is no means of producing music and, for the moment, the Sibelius can exist only in my mind.

Not so the Sauna. In Finland, the sauna is a national institution and it is clear that nothing further is going to happen until we have partaken. Ulla, Pertti's young assistant, has cooked us a beautiful meal but, when saunas are concerned, eating has to wait.

At the edge of the lake stands a little wooden hut, a plume of smoke curling up from its chimney. This is the venue for the coming event. Ulla has been stoking the fire all afternoon and everything is in readiness. Pertti says that he and I are to go first while Margaret and Ulla will come for the second sitting.

We walk to the hut, he opens the door and a blast of saharan heat hits us. Outside the late afternoon is sharply cool but, within seconds, the sweat is pouring out of me. We strip off all our clothes and sit on a wooden bench while I wonder what temperature is required to produce heat stroke. There is more to come. On top of the fire is a large drum of stones, heated to furnace temperature. Beside it stands a tub of water and Pertti now scoops up a ladleful and throws it on the stones. There is a violent hiss and I gasp as my lungs fill with superheated steam, which feels as though it will burn away their linings.

We sit there while the sweat runs, Pertti tips more water onto the stones and the temperature seems to go even higher. Suddenly he says, "Now we can go to the lake", opens the door, runs down the little jetty and leaps in.

I believe that Finns and Swedes have an unusually high incidence of heart attack. Now, it seems, I perhaps know why. However, the family honour is at stake and I follow him in. If the heat of the sauna has been intense, then the cold of the lake is something beyond this. I manage three strokes out and then three back, emerging as chilled with cold as I have been burning with heat only seconds before.

For the rest of our stay, Pertti frequently says, "We must take another sauna." Strangely, we never take him up on it. In the morning, it will be off to the spruce forests and the Ural Owl.

The Ural Owl! The owl that attacks by day! Many owls are fearless protectors of their breeding territories, readily striking any human intruder who ventures too close to nest or young. However, these assaults usually take place under cover of darkness and there are only a few species who will do so in daylight. Among these are the two big owls of Europe's northern forests, the Great Grey and the Ural.

An attack by a Ural Owl is equally both a frightening and an exhilarating experience. Ural Owls do nothing to hide their feelings. It is always the female which does the attacking, usually when she has large young.

She greets the trespasser at once with obvious displeasure, snapping her bill, barking and then flying to a high and prominent perch where she can have an unimpeded view of her target. Woe betide the human observer who takes his eyes off her from then on. Owls much prefer surprise attacks and are past masters at timing them to coincide with a lapse in concentration on the part of their intended target.

Pertti wraps his arms around the trunk of the spruce tree and starts to climb. It is a warm day but he wears a heavy leather jacket, thick fur hat with ear-flaps and a full-face perspex visor. Torn and frayed, the jacket bears the scars of many previous encounters with the owls.

PREVIOUS PAGE
Ural Owl. A female keeps watch over her nest and the human intruder.
TOP
Climbing to a Tengmalm's Owl box under the watchful eye of the female. For this inoffensive bird, there is no need to wear head protection.
BOTTOM
Pertti checking the female at a Ural Owl nestbox. For this fearsomely aggressive species, he is wearing full protective headgear.

Six metres above him is the wooden nest box, its rounded entrance hole facing out over the forest. There are three owlets in the nest, part-feathered and within a few days of leaving their birthplace.

Pertti is halfway to the box when the owl launches herself into a long glide. Her broad wings and absence of flapping make her flight look slow and it is only when she is nearly on him that her speed is apparent. He ducks, covering his face, the owl's talons strike his back with great force and then she is lifting away to a new perch across the clearing. Pertti has experienced it many times before and scarcely checks his climb but the owl's talons have pierced his jacket and the effects on an eye, a face or an unprotected back would have been very different.

This pair of Ural Owls is one of several thousand using nest boxes in the forests of southern Finland. These nest boxes are a story in themselves. Historically, much of Finland had been covered in extensive pine forests; old forests with hollow trees and snapped-off stumps, both of which provided nest sites for the large owls.

Modern timber practices have changed this radically and, although much of the forest still remains, the old trees have been culled, the forest is much younger and very few potential nest trees remain. The owls' future was looking decidedly bleak when, nearly fifty years ago, Pertti began his study and realised what was happening. It was already too late to save many of the old trees and it seemed that the only way to save the owls was going to be to provide them with alternative nest sites.

So began the nest box project, a scheme which was embarked on with such enthusiasm that there are now over ten thousand Ural Owl nest boxes spread through the forests of southern Finland and a further ten thousand for the smaller species of owl which are similarly threatened, the Tawny, Tengmalm's and Pygmy. It has been a huge effort but its success can be gauged by the fact that, in 1994, over three hundred pairs of Ural Owls were using nest boxes in Pertti's personal study area alone. A few pairs were still breeding in natural sites but, without the nest boxes, the Ural Owl would clearly have become a very scarce bird.

The Ural Owl project started as a rescue mission but it also presented a marvellous opportunity for a scientific study. Unlike birds in natural nests, the boxes are all at known sites, are placed at an easy height for climbing and have access to the inside through removable lids. A detachable trapping box can be fitted to the front and, with this, it is possible to detain an adult when it returns to the nest.

OPPOSITE
Waiting for their bands. Three
nestling URAL OWLS at the
foot of the nest tree
FOLLOWING PAGE
Flight through the forest
– a URAL OWL at night

Pertti is a dedicated scientist and head of bird ringing for the whole of Finland. Since 1964, these birds have been his project. Each year, he visits every nest box to see if there are owls in residence. Then, for every occupied one, he must return when there are young. They are ringed, weighed and measured. The identity of the mother is checked and then, later, the father. It is a huge task for most of it must be done in just four weeks when the young are in the nest. It is just as well that this happens at a season of almost perpetual daylight for there is little time for sleep and, at least, it is possible to work at all times with fair visibility.

If the task is great, then so are the results and Pertti's knowledge of his owl population would rival that of any government census of people; homes occupied, homes vacant, sizes of clutches, numbers of young with lengths and weights, identity of father, age of mother, deaths, marriages and divorces. It is all there, a vast bank of information, which is of great benefit to the owls themselves as well as to the scientists.

113116 is a male Ural Owl. He first appeared as a breeding bird in 1992, married to female 126182. They raised families in 1992 and 1993 before she moved to a new nest box and, for a while, he disappeared. However, their relationship was not over and, in 1996, he followed her to the new nest site.

Now the plot thickens for, in that year, 126182 was not his only wife. He had taken a second mate, 156437, who was occupying his 1992 site. Both females laid eggs with the second female's clutch a few days later than the other's. All went well until the eggs hatched when the male's difficulties in hunting for two sets of young began to emerge. He provided well for the first wife's brood but, gradually, brought less and less prey to the second nest. Finally, with the two young only a few days old, 156437 had to start hunting herself, leaving the chicks, which still needed her warmth, alone in the nest. She made a valiant effort and managed to rear one but it was at the expense of the smaller chick. Pertti was watching their progress carefully and, day by day, the small one's growth fell steadily behind until, at just under three weeks, it died

The following year, 113116 continued his bigamous career with the same two females. 126182 stayed in the same place while 156437 moved to a new nest site but he followed her there and again found himself providing for two broods. This time, however, it was 156437 who had become the favourite wife and whose young were fed first. Nevertheless, 126182 was not completely abandoned and both females were able to raise their broods.

For 126182 it was the end of the marriage and 113116 did not breed with her again. 156437 became his only wife and they moved back to their original

nest site, the same one that he had first used in 1992. Interestingly, the other two sites, which flanked his territory, were now both occupied by his sons, married to two sisters of different lineage. It seemed almost that the younger members of the family had decided that they had to exercise some sort of control over their errant father.

Margaret and I spent a week with Pertti in that spring of 1994, a week when I saw more nesting owls than I had done in the whole of my previous ten years of owling. Seven years later, we came again but this story concerns mainly the first visit.

A Finnish forest in May is a place of softness and silence. Thick, spongy moss carpets the ground and very little wind filters down through the closely packed spruce trees. At the edge of the forest there are birches and Scots Pines but these are essentially spruce forests and it is difficult to find any other species once inside. There is no under-storey but the greens and browns of the forest floor are bejewelled with the brilliant blues and whites of massed anemones.

As we approached the angular shape of the first nest box, I thought how incongruous this man-made structure looked amid the almost pristine beauty of the forest. Still, the owls owed their very being to its presence.

There was no sign of an owl but, from inside the box, came a sound like the single snapping of castanets, the bill-snapping threat display of the female. During the next few days, we would come to know this sound well.

This was a particularly stoical female and she had small young. She held her ground as Pertti climbed the tree, making no attempt to escape when he raised the lid of the box and lifted her off the chicks. Her ring showed that she was an old occupant of this box but her young were too small to ring yet. As we walked away, she was still inside, snapping her displeasure.

The owner of the next box was also inside but Pertti knew that she was a shyer bird and unlikely to stay there as he climbed. Also, she had no ring so it was essential to catch her. The ingenious method involved the use of a fifteen-metre pole with a wad of soft cloth on the end, like a boxing glove attached to en extremely long arm. The technique consisted of approaching the tree as silently as possible and then thrusting the wadded end of the pole into the nest entrance. It calls for considerable dexterity and a certain amount of luck and, on this occasion, it failed. The owl sensed the approaching danger and flew as Pertti manoeuvred his trembling pole into position. This bird would have to be caught in a different way.

Neither of these owls had shown more than token aggression but the next

two females quickly changed that perception. As we walked to the first one, we heard bill-snapping and then her short double bark which serves both as an alarm and as a food soliciting call to the male. Moments later, she glided through the forest and perched in full view, staring at us fixedly. We knew that we were in for trouble.

This owl made twenty one strikes on Pertti in the short time that he was up the tree, raking him with her talons as she came in from every angle. With his experience and protective gear, this was thrilling but harmless but it could have been a different story at night or with a surprise attack. Owls are fascinating birds but they also have the ability to be extremely dangerous and no owl watcher should ever forget that.

At the next nest, Pertti lowered the young to the ground for Ulla to take weights and measurements and the attacks were more ferocious still. Pertti was the initial object of the female's ire but, when the young came to ground, she switched her attentions to Ulla who, lacking protection, had a very uncomfortable time as she carried out her tasks.

At this nest, we still had to catch and radio tag the male. For this we needed Gunnar. Gunnar was a stuffed Ural Owl who had come from the Swedish museum in Stockholm. He is also a character in a Finnish song, a ram, who comes in from a foreign country and tries to mate with all the ewes. The name was apt.

Gunnar's perch was atop a large loudspeaker, itself mounted on a tall tripod. This was set up in a clearing, flanked on two sides by forest. Behind him were two long mist nets, four metres high, set up at right angles to each other. The Ural Owls were nesting in that piece of forest and the trap was set. Fifty metres away, Pertti sat with the loudspeaker controls and waited for dusk.

It was 11-0 p.m. before the light had faded sufficiently. Pertti switched on the tape and the calls began; low, short, triple hoots with the middle note slightly higher than the other two. It sounded wonderfully realistic and so too did the sight of Gunnar, perched outside the forest in the twilight.

The reply came almost at once and the resident male glided to a high perch overlooking Gunnar, big, broad-winged and powerful. He called again and Gunnar called back, not flying away as an intruding male should have done. Clearly puzzled, the male flew to another perch and then another, proclaiming his sovereignty at each new stopping point. The steadfast Gunnar called back.

It took fifteen minutes for the attack to come. He came in steeply, gliding over the top of the first mist net to strike Gunnar a shuddering blow. When the feathers had settled, a dishevelled Gunnar was still on his perch but his assailant was caught, his talons ensnared in the mesh of the mist net. Pertti

OPPOSITE
The ever curious Tengmalm's Owl peers down from her nest in an old Black Woodpecker hole

raced to free him before he became entangled further. Then followed the measuring, weighing, banding and radio tagging, none of which impressed the owl, who snapped his bill constantly in disapproval. Finally, we were able to release him and he was away and back into the forest, at once setting up an indignant hooting which seemed likely to continue for hours.

Although Ural Owls were our main objective, we also visited nests of Tengmalm's, Pygmy and Great Grey Owls.

Tengmalm's is a relatively small owl and able to squeeze into old Black Woodpecker holes, making it less dependent on artificial sites than the Ural. Two of such sites were in birches, soft-trunked trees that are much favoured by woodpeckers. Characteristically, the females peered out at us in response to a little scratching on the tree. Many owls ignore tree scratching but Tengmalm's seem to be innately curious and unable to resist the temptation to see who is causing the disturbance. This appearance is reinforced by their facial expressions, big eyes and raised eyebrows creating a look of constant surprise.

The tiny Pygmy Owl is almost a diurnal bird, often awake and hunting throughout the day and rarely active during the darkest part of the night. The female was incubating a huge clutch of nine eggs, an indication of the rigours of life in these latitudes for, despite these numbers, the Pygmy Owl is not a common bird. Unlike the similar-sized but insectivorous European Scops Owl, the Pygmy Owl does not migrate. It is a hunter of birds and small mammals, many of them nearly as big as itself and winter must be a very hard season for it.

On the first night, I arrived at the nest at ten o'clock and was too late. It was still nearly two hours until sunset but there would be little darkness that night. The male was there with prey and I heard his soft, musical whistle as he called to the female. She replied with a single thin whistle, almost too high to hear, and flew straight to him. I could not see the prey transfer but it was quick and she wasted no time in returning, diving straight into the tiny entrance, giving me no chance either to fire the camera or name the prey.

An hour later, the male was back again in a carbon copy of the first visit. I fired the flashes but the female was already through and I saw only the nest entrance, ice-cold batteries having slowed the camera's response time to half a second.

That was the start of a very long wait and it was nearly 4·0 a.m., well after sunrise, before the male returned. During that time, I watched the sun's afterglow move slowly across the northern sky on a night that never grew darker than twilight. I think he brought food but could not be sure and when, for the third time, the female dived headlong into the nest, I took my leave.

OPPOSITE
Tengmalm's Owl. The incubating female stayed on the eggs while we lifted the lid of the nest box to look inside
FOLLOWING PAGE LEFT
Tengmalm's Owl, one of the most attractive of all owls.
FOLLOWING PAGE RIGHT
European Pygmy Owl at the entrance to her nest hollow

The next night I was there earlier and much better prepared. At ten o'clock the female left the nest, quite silently. It was an exercise flight, such as many owls take and she would be away for only a few minutes. During her absence, I heard tiny squeaks coming from within the hollow. At least some of the chicks had hatched out.

Sometimes a wildlife photographer must resort to a little subterfuge to induce his subject to cooperate. Now, while the female was away, I pushed a little plug of moss into the entrance. Hopefully, this would cause her to delay just long enough for my purpose.

Not a wisp of moss was showing outside the hole but the returning owl could see and she flew past three times before landing on the lip. Puzzled, she put her head in the hole and pulled at the moss. It moved, but only a little and she drew back, looking round, before trying again but still without success. By now, she was growing impatient and changed her tactic, thrusting her whole head into the hole and pushing. It worked and she tumbled into the nest, taking the moss with her.

Half an hour later, she took another flight and it was eleven o'clock before the male arrived with food. He brought a vole and she took it straight in to the young. The entrance was too tight for owl and prey to go in together and she went through first, leaving one foot hanging onto the vole to drag it through the entrance behind. It was nearly midnight and, not having the stamina for another 4·0 a.m. session, I headed home.

The Great Grey Owl is one of the mythical owls of the north, a fearsome bird whose great size belies its small bulk. It appears almost as big as an Eagle Owl but much of this is down and feathers and it is less then half the Eagle Owls' weight, making it highly vulnerable to predation by the larger owl. There is a purpose for this dense feathering for the Great Grey Owl is one of the few birds which can withstand winter in these forests, insulated by its feathers from the intense cold and with such acute, directional hearing that it is able to capture small mammals in total darkness as they move beneath the snow. The initial detection is usually from a listening perch and then the owl launches into a shallow glide, beaming in on the unsuspecting prey to plunge its talons deep into the snow, often leaving an imprint of its wings in the snow as evidence of the capture.

To see the Great Grey Owl, we travelled to the easternmost part of Finland and into Karelia, a region immortalised by Sibelius in his Karelia Suite. It is a disputed region, for part of it was seized by the Russians in 1918 and Finnish pride has never accepted this as permanent. I had only a few hours with the

OPPOSITE, TOP
The entrance to the Pygmy Owl's hole was so tight that she had to enter first and drag her vole prey in behind her
OPPOSITE, BOTTOM
This incubating Pygmy Owl is using a nest box

TOP
Great Grey Owl, the great
owl of the northern forests
BOTTOM
The incubating owl glared at
me from the depths of her
huge facial disc

owls, which were using an old raptor's nest, ten metres up in a Silver Birch tree.

The female watched us as we approached, peering over the rim of the nest with tiny yellow eyes set in the ringed feathers of the huge facial disc. Hearing is all-important to Great Grey Owls and the eyes play little part in hunting. There was a Scots Pine near the nest tree, which offered me a chance to climb level with the nest and my eyes never left the bird as I went up, mindful of the species reputation for attacking. She made no move and then, when Pertti began climbing the nest tree to check the eggs, slipped quietly off the nest and flew away. It seemed that this Great Grey was not going to live up to the species' reputation.

Throughout the world, owls have the effect of exciting fury among other birds and, almost at once, the Magpies and Fieldfares found her and began mobbing furiously. Margaret followed her to an exposed, low perch but, by the time I had climbed down my tree, the birds had driven her further away. I did manage to take a couple of pictures but the eggs were exposed and vulnerable and it would have been very unwise to keep her off. As we began to walk away, she was already working her way back towards the nest.

We had only a week with Pertti and could have done with a month. Southern Finland is also Eagle Owl country, biggest and most powerful owl of all. During our stay, we were shown three active nests, all on the ground and all with young; wonderful subjects to photograph. It could not be. Eagle Owls cannot be studied in a hurry and would clearly need a future expedition all to themselves.

Our second visit in 2001 was as fascinating as the first and there were two notable additions. The first was the presence of Pertti's wife, Hemuli. In 1994, she had been unable to come and her presence added grace and charm to our time at Hauho, Pertti's forest retreat. The second was our meeting with the Capercaillie, the huge forest grouse of Europe's northern forests.

In spring, male Capercaillies become aggressively territorial, guarding their kingdoms with furious intensity against other males while attracting females from all around the district to come and mate. Pertti's friend, Pekka Poiku, knows one Capercaillie very well, so well that he has persuaded it that he himself is a rival male.

With Pekka, we went to a clearing in the forest, the centre of the Capercaillie's territory. We had no need to search for him. As we arrived, he appeared, only 40 metres away, strutting up and down among the moss and boulders, proclaiming his sovereignty. He was a dramatic sight, big and glossy black with fiery red eyebrows, shining green head plumes, neck and beak stretched skywards and the tail raised and spread like a turkey cock.

I expected him to run off but Pekka and the bird knew each other well and they were rivals. Pekka walked towards him, waving his arms like wings and then turned to run away, crouching and lifting the tail of his coat. From the outset, the Capercaillie had been threatening him, not only through bodily manner but also with strange clicking and belching sounds, which were clearly aggressive in intent. Now he ran at Pekka, pecking furiously at his boots and then flying up at his body in a flurry of wings and beak.

I had been resting my camera on a log to record the action and, suddenly, the bird switched his attentions to me, jumping up on the log and coming straight at me. The power of the attack was amazing and I was glad that I had the advantage of size. He left me and returned to his strutting and belching before launching a second attack on Pekka, and then another one. Probably this could have gone on for a long time but we could have caused an unnecessary drain on his energies so we granted him victory and left. It was a fitting end to our second visit to the forests of Finland, forests which I could visit a score of times and still find wonder and fascination.

RIGHT
Play Acting. Margaret with a captured Ural Owl which lay on its' back and feigned death. Moments later, it rolled over and flew away.
OPPOSITE, FAR RIGHT & BOTTOM
Ural Owls are not the only aggressive inhabitants of a Finnish forest. A male Capercaillie shows his displeasure at our presence before launching an attack on Pekka Poiku

Japan

Blakiston's Fish Owl

An owl that lives by catching fish! I had long been fascinated that such a bird could exist; hunting in the darkness; seeking prey that makes no sound; coping with the problems of reflection, refraction and the blackness of water in the night. My journeys would not be complete until I had seen one.

There are two groups of owls in the world that catch fish, the Fishing Owls of Africa and the Fish Owls of Asia, closely related but, at the moment, classified in two separate genera, Scotopelia and Ketupa.

In 1991, I went to the Okavango River in Botswana, hoping to learn something of Pel's Fishing Owl, the most widespread of the three African fishing owls. In an eight day stay, I did see two owls but I learned quickly that these birds are extremely shy, flying from their daytime riverside roosts at the very first glimpse of a distant, approaching human. Reputedly, they are more approachable at night when perched over the water in search of fish. I travelled the river after dark with boat and spotlight, picking up a wide variety of birds and animals but, if Pel's Owl was there, it did not show itself.

In 1995, I turned my attention to Malaysia and to the Buffy Fish Owl, one of the three fish owls of South-east Asia. My guide knew of only one pair but assured me that it was always possible to find them in their territory outside Kuala Lumpur. There are no certainties with wildlife and, in the week that I was with him, there was not a trace of them. My only Buffy Fish Owl sighting was of a bird in the Kuala Lumpur Zoo, a tantalising glimpse that only strengthened my wish to see a fish owl in the wild. The determination was there but the opportunity seemed as far away as ever.

Then my Finnish friend Pertti Saurola told me of Sumio Yamamoto in Japan, the world's greatest expert on Blakiston's Fish Owl. I wrote to Sumio and he replied at once, saying that he would be delighted to have me visit him.

I could hardly credit my good fortune. Blakiston's Fish Owl is a singular bird in many ways. Not only is it a fish owl but it is also the largest owl in the world, exceeding even the biggest races of the European Eagle Owl. Thomas Blakiston, British consul in Hokkaido, gave the species its' name and wrote the first description, late in the nineteenth century. It is a very northerly bird, living in regions where most of the rivers are frozen in winter, a serious drawback for a bird which lives by catching fish. Finally, it is extremely rare and probably critically endangered, limited to a few hundred pairs in eastern Siberia and an even smaller number on the Japanese island of Hokkaido and the adjacent Kurile Islands. I had never even considered that I might have a chance to work with it.

In November 2002, I set off from Australia with my old friend Alan Cowan, who had been with me on the Alaskan trip. We flew first to Tokyo, a vast city where, despite the huge crush of humanity, there is an overwhelming impression of order and efficiency with everything seeming to work and to be on time. We had been concerned at our total ignorance of the language but the Japanese have long ago overcome this problem and it was easier to find our way than in many English-speaking cities. From there, we flew on to Kushiro in Hokkaido, the most northerly of Japan's main islands. Waiting at the airport gate, was our genial host.

Sumio Yamamoto is a remarkable man. For 30 years, he has devoted his life to the welfare, conservation and study of Blakiston's Fish Owl, a marathon of application and dedication that few could rival. Not only is he the world's greatest expert on the species but, under his stewardship, there has been a gradual recovery in Hokkaido's fish owl numbers from less than 30 birds in 1983 to the present population of about 50 pairs with a further 30 juvenile and non-breeding birds. He has had some help but he is the driving force behind it all and the vast majority of the work and the success is due to him. Notwithstanding all this, he has also written a book on Blakiston's Fish Owl, a superb monograph, beautifully illustrated with his own photographs. Reading it is, for most of us, complicated by the text being in Japanese but there are lengthy English captions to all the pictures, which go a long way to overcoming the language difficulty.

We drove east towards the fishing port of Nemuro at the eastern tip of Hokkaido. It was November and already cold. We were on about the same latitude as Barcelona but the two climates are vastly different and the geography books describe the one here as sub-arctic. Certainly the vegetation fitted this label with boreal forest of birch and pines, interspersed with dairying pasture. Already, the deciduous trees were quite bare of leaves. Strangely, and almost incongruously, we at once started to see numbers of Black Kites, a species which I have always associated with the crowded cities of tropical Asia and the arid inland of Australia.

It was dark when Sumio dropped us at the guesthouse which would be our base for the next week. Our hosts, Masaru Takata and his wife Sako were a delight. This was a traditional Japanes guesthouse with two-tiered dormitories and the communal hot tub, filled with steaming water at all hours of the day. Perhaps not everything, we felt, was completely typical. Masaru is himself a bird man, widely travelled and the author of several children's natural history books. His English is excellent and the familiar spines of two Australian field

guides were conspicuous on his bookshelves. His business card describes him as "Master of Furoso Field Inn", a title which we seized upon for some good-humoured banter for, if anything, it is Sako who is the master, a superb cook who produced one delightful Japanese meal after another. She is also a jam maker, surely not a Japanese tradition, and we were treated each day to a selection of 24 varieties, all prepared from wild fruits which she had gathered in the surrounding countryside.

In the morning, Sumio called and we headed for the forest. We came first to the edge of Lake Furen, a big and shallow sea-lake with a narrow opening to the ocean. Around its' shores was the spectacular sight of huge numbers of Whooper Swans, recently arrived from the Arctic. Mostly, they were gleaming white adults but there was a proportion of dark grey cygnets too, only recently out of down but having already made the long flight south with their parents. Soon the lakes would freeze and the swans would be forced to fly further south still.

Then we arrived at a locked gate, Sumio opened it and we were in the forest. Like so many parts of the world, Hokkaido has been stripped of most of its' original native forest and what remains is mostly re-growth or has been planted. Nevertheless, it is vital habitat and much of it is very carefully protected in wildlife reserves. Here too, the rivers still follow their natural courses, not confined within steep-sided canals as they are through much of Japan. For the fish owls, this is vital.

Most of the forest was evergreen conifer interspersed with patches of Japanese Oak and Silver Birch along the gullies. The track ran down to a river flat where the other trees gave place to Alders. None of the trees was big enough to form hollows and on one of them was a huge cylindrical nest box. Just as in Finland, the owls are now dependent on man-made nest sites to survive.

At the edge of the river was a strong, steel-mesh enclosure, open to the sky and with a small pool inside, fed by the river. Sumio stocks this with small trout each day and, from the evidence of the thick whitewash below some of the overlooking perches, the owls were making good use of it. He took a net and, from an adjacent holding tank, used it to scoop up fresh supplies of fish and transfer them to the pool.

We left the enclosure and walked into the forest, along the river and then up a spur. The ground was carpeted thickly with moss and I thought how like the forests of Finland it seemed. We were half-way up the spur when Sumio exclaimed "Fish Owl" and I looked across a gully to see the biggest owl that I had ever seen. Even against my recollection of the European Eagle Owl, this bird looked enormous. It was perched on the horizontal limb of a leafless tree, barely 60 metres away and was acutely alert. It was accustomed to Sumio, who usually came alone, but here were three people and its' huge ear tufts were raised in alarm, projecting upwards and outwards at 45 degrees.

If this had been an Eagle Owl, it would have been gone long before but this bird just watched us, exchanging stare for stare. It was a pale, tawny-brown bird with brilliant yellow eyes and the startlingly prominent ear tufts, which can be raised or lowered at will. In many ways, these perform the same function as facial expression in humans, able to show fear, anger, concentration and tranquility. It takes muscular effort to raise them and they are of no benefit to the resting bird or when hunting, when they could easily get in the way, so, at these times, they lie flat on the head and are barely visible.

I had ample time to take in the rest of its' details. On the breast and belly there was fine, wavy, brown barring, superimposed with long black streaks, while the upper wings were a complex chequerboard of browns and white. The tail looked short, while the legs were completely enveloped by the puffed out feathers of the belly, surrounding them like an insulating muff so that only the huge blue talons were visible, curled around the branch. Sumio said that this was the female.

It was raining and the light was poor but I might never get a chance again and raced back to the car to fetch the camera. It took ten minutes but she had not moved and I took some pictures in light that was hardly suited to long lens photography.

She would have stayed but then the Jungle Crows found her. I heard the deep, Raven-like "Krok Krok" as the first one appeared. It was a big crow, almost as big as a European Raven and with a similarly massive bill. It perched on a limb several metres above the owl, threatening, but she ignored it. Then, however, other Jungle Crows heard the disturbance and began to arrive, all intent on harassing the owl. Within a few minutes, there were nearly 20, all shouting their disapproval, yet never daring to venture too close. Finally, the owl had had enough. In the manner of all big owls, she turned very slowly, paused and launched herself. Even having noted the size of the bird, I was astounded at the spread of the huge, broad wings, which span a full two metres.

Sumio said that this was fish owl territory No.4. He had four territories that he knew intimately and visited daily. There was a similarity between them all with a small river running for between 10 and 15 kilometres through a narrow strip of forest, a kilometre or less in width. This pair had raised two young that season in the nest box that we had just seen.

We left the forest and drove on to the next territory a few kilometres away.

TOP
The people of Nemuro care
about their owls. Road sign to
ask people to drive carefully
to avoid hitting an owl
BOTTOM
Road bridge near Nemuro.
The banners are there for the
specific purpose of forcing
Blakiston's Fish Owls to fly high
and avoid being hit by traffic

At the approaches to a river bridge on the main road, there was a bright yellow owl sign and then the superstructure of the bridge was adorned on both sides with vertical yellow banners, two metres high, half a metre wide and arranged closely together. I assumed that this was part of some festival but Sumio told us that he had persuaded the roads department to put them there to force the owls to fly high over the road and avoid being hit by the traffic, a fate which had previously befallen several of them. It is this devotion to his cause and determination to see his recommendations carried out which have just started to turn the tide for the fish owls. One or two fish owls killed by cars does not sound much but, in a population which may produce only 10 to 15 young each year, it is highly significant.

Sumio has also succeeded in having horizontal perching bars fitted above the tops of the electricity power poles, another life-saving measure, particularly as the fish owls have a liking for these elevated perches. His enthusiasm is infectious and, during the week, I came to realise how much interest there is among the local people, both in the owls and in some of the other spectacular species of birds which occur there.

At territory No 1, we again entered through a locked gate. These precious pieces of forest are very carefully protected. The track lead down through the trees to a shallow gully and a tiny pool, only a few metres across and, at that time, almost empty, for the creek was not flowing. With an electric pump and pipe, Sumio is able to fill this and then stock it with trout, which are kept from escaping by a low shingle bank at the outlet of the pool. Every day, he replenishes this and similar pools in his other territories with fish, a technique which ensures that his owls' nutrition is always good, enabling them to breed every year. In many seasons, his birds produce two young while, elsewhere in Hokkaido, other pairs may not breed every year and, when they do, produce one young or none at all. It is this slow injection of new, young birds which is gradually lifting the Hokkaido population from the brink of extinction. Sumio already had a hide in place and, in the evening, I was to come to this pool to watch.

Here, at No 1, was a different forest, made up entirely of deciduous trees and with the ground densely carpeted with Sasa, a dwarf bamboo which varied from ankle height to above the knee. The leafless trees allowed good visibility but it was the owl which saw us first, launching its' huge wings through the forest and away when we were still 300 metres off. "Female" said Sumio. "This one is always shy." Moments later, two more owls flew and followed her. "Juveniles" Sumio said. How he could tell I am not sure for, to me, they all seemed just about identical. This was one of two pairs which had raised two young that season. We walked on. Sumio had already said that this male was not shy and so it turned out to be. He was 200 metres away when we saw him but he allowed us closer and closer until I was looking up from less than 20 metres away. It was a thrilling sight but the grey light and white sky were hardly the best for photography. There was no point in forcing him to fly and we walked quietly away.

That evening, with high expectations, I settled into the hide beside the pool. It was raining and with the sound of this, plus the distant traffic, I was concerned that I might not hear the owl arrive. From close by came a shrill, descending cry, reminiscent of both the Sooty Owl and the Bush Stone-curlew of Australia but not quite right for either. I knew it was not the fish owl but had no idea of its' origin. Later, Sumio told me that this was the voice of the Shika Deer, a common animal in the forest. I stayed for three hours but there was no sign of the fish owl.

In the night, the rain stopped and the temperature fell. By morning, a thin fringe of ice had appeared round the edges of the lakes and the ground was hard underfoot. In places, the ice cracked and tinkled as we walked. We went first to Territory 4, where we had seen the owl yesterday. She was nowhere to be found and we followed the river downstream, beyond where we had been before.

Just round the first bend, we came upon the murder scene, a broad area of churned-up sand, a mass of trampled feathers and the remains of one of the great owls, reduced to a crumpled heap of bones and feathers. The wings were there, almost intact, together with the skull, the beak and the curling talons, all still connected to a skeleton from which all flesh had been removed. The pale colouring revealed this bird as a juvenile, one of the two which this pair had reared in the spring. Clearly there had been a struggle but the owl had succumbed.

This was a big blow and Sumio was visibly upset. With the owls in such a precarious situation, the death of even one young bird is a big loss. He said that a fox or a raccoon was almost certainly the culprit. Foxes are native to Hokkaido but not so raccoons, brought over as pets from North America and then, by accident or design, let loose in the wild. As with so many feral animals around the world, they are running rampant and are particularly dangerous in that, unlike the fox, they can climb, placing the nests of even the largest birds at risk.

We saw no more owls that day and, when I returned to the hide by the pool, it was already freezing. A first-quarter moon shone in front of me, dipping slowly to the horizon. The sky was clear and it was quite still.

OPPOSITE, TOP
Sumio Yamamoto and Alan Cowan standing in Sasa, the dwarf bamboo which carpets many of the forests of Hokkaido.
OPPOSITE, BOTTOM
Sumio with the dead fish owl, killed by either a fox or the introduced raccoon

It was half an hour after sunset when the first owl arrived. The previous night, I had been concerned that I would not hear it but I need not have worried. Silent flight is not one of Blakiston's Fish Owl's attributes and it was still some way off when I heard the thrashing of great wings and then a crash as it tried to land on a rotten branch above the pool, snapping it off to send it tumbling into the water while the owl flailed on. When the noise stopped, I knew that it had perched and was not far away.

For a few minutes, there was silence. Then the owl flew and landed again, still in the trees and out of my sight but now quite close. Moments later, the huge form glided down and pitched on a log beside the pool, only six metres from me. It was a magical moment. To have this great, mystical bird, perched of its' own volition and almost within touching distance, was one of those exquisite happenings which make owls the most special of birds. All remnants of daylight had gone but the moon touched the outline of its' feathers, tracing the dark shadow with a fine rim of silver which was just enough for me to make out its' shape. The moon also put the faintest light from the sky onto the water so that I could dimly make out the owl's reflection, jutting out as a dark, rounded shape into the fading pool of light.

I waited and the owl waited, both of us still and silent in the darkness. It was too dark to focus or frame the bird and, finally, I decided to risk it and show a glimmer of torch. Perhaps this bird was the female, the shy one, for she did not like it, turning slowly, then looking skywards and flying. I cursed myself, then realised that she had not gone far and, within five minutes, she dropped back to the log while I kept my hand off the torch.

She had been there for minutes only when there was the sound of more owl wings and a second bird arrived, first in the trees, then dropping down to the near side of the pool, even closer to me than the first one. I think this was the male. Then I heard wings for a third time and it seemed that the whole fish owl family was gathering. I shone the torch, at first right away from them but then gradually closer. The female looked but stayed where she was, while the male took no notice at all. Just as with our very first bird, I again noted the great depth of feathering around the lower body, spread out in a dense, insulating skirt, completely obscuring the legs. In the climate where these birds live, it is an understandable adaptation.

The male was intent on fishing, leaning forward, lowering his head and peering into the water. It did not take long. He waded forward, paused and then pounced, striking with his feet while balancing himself with waving wings. I could not see if he used both feet or one but he had a 20 centimetre fish in his bill, held by the head and dangling vertically down. He raised his head, gulped and it was gone. Five minutes later, he caught another one with an identical technique. For the moment, it seemed that this was enough. He flew but I knew that he had not gone far and, when I left the hide, he was perched on a branch a short distance above me.

It was 7·0 pm when Sumio returned. The female was still beside the pool but flew when she heard him coming. I crawled out of the hide and the male owl was still above me, perched where he had flown on leaving the pool. Now came the most unexpected event of all. Sumio took a net and walked to the pool to retrieve the remaining fish. There would be little water left there by morning. He was standing there when the owl dropped from the tree, landed also at the water's edge and at once began looking for fish with Sumio standing only three metres away. It was a remarkable demonstration of the relationship which had developed between owl and man, a relationship which, admittedly, was based on food but was no less notable for that.

For the next two days we gave both Sumio and the owls a rest and, with a guide, set out to see some of the other birds of south-eastern Hokkaido. It is an area which is famous for its' Japanese Cranes and for the great winter congregations of Steller's Sea-eagles, one of the rarest and most spectacular eagles in the world.

Already, it was late in the season for the cranes. Japanese Cranes breed around Nemuro but, when the swamps and rivers freeze, they move a short distance west to Kushiro where the rivers come down from the mountains, run more swiftly and do not freeze. The need is not so much for an unfrozen place to feed as for an unfrozen place to roost, standing with their legs in icy water where they are safe from the attention of foxes.

We saw several pairs and one family party of three, tall, elegant and very beautiful. Their gleaming white body feathers are made even more startling by the jet-black neck, black legs and the long, tertiary wing feathers, which flop down over the tail like a bustle. The dagger-like bill is bright yellow and only the red of the crown is difficult to make out, except in the very best light.

The people of Hokkaido are very proud of their cranes. They are the emblem of the city of Kushiro whose main bridge is adorned with four beautiful crane sculptures, one on each corner. On Lake Furen, overlooking the crane breeding marshes, the restaurants provide high quality telescopes and binoculars for the diners to watch the birds, while the nearby environmental centre is similarly equipped.

The winter assemblies of Steller's Sea-eagles around Nemuro are also legendary. There, in February, the temperatures drop to between −20°C and −40°C, the sea is frozen and the sea lakes are covered in ice so thick that it

TOP
Ural Owl, an unexpected
lodger in the vacant nest hole
of a Blakiston's Fish Owl
BOTTOM
Japanese Crane, a very special
bird in the Nemuro district

will stand the weight of a truck. For centuries, the professional fishermen have fished throughout the winter, cutting circular holes in the ice to gain access to the water. They catch four species of fish, three of which they can sell while the fourth one is useless to them. These are discarded and the sea-eagles have long known of this so that they have come to rely on them to survive through the winter. On frozen Lake Furen, there may be as many as 600 Steller's Sea-eagles at one time, so intent on the fish that they ignore the fishermen completely.

We were too early for this sight but, with luck, we might see one of the early arrivals. We were half way down the narrow, eastward-pointing Notsuki Peninsula when it appeared, flying low and coming directly towards us. If there is a more spectacular eagle in the world, then I have yet to see it. It was a huge eagle with dramatically white forewings and a brilliant orange-yellow bill, quite monstrous in size, and a gleaming yellow eye behind it. Apart from the bill and the yellow legs, it was a white and black bird; white forewings and tail, both above and below, white thighs and the rest of the plumage black. The tail was deeply wedged. It sailed close past, looking but without any suggestion of changing course to take it away from us. The next day, we saw one at the edge of a forest overlooking a lake, perched on the very top of the crown of the biggest pine where all the world could see it, the king of this environment without any need for concealment.

The Nemuro district is a region of fishing villages, which abound with gulls of many kinds, sometimes with eight species present in one small harbour. For an Australian, accustomed to only two species, it was a strange sight. Some groups of resting birds were made up of five species of varying ages, an excellent chance to note subtle differences.

On the sixth day, we were back with Sumio. Not all of his Blakiston's Fish Owls use artificial nests and he took us to see two natural sites. The first one, overlooking a lake and a swamp, was in the top of the trunk of a big, snapped-off Japanese Oak, a cavity which was almost a metre deep but was open to the sky, the type of site which is well-liked by Great Grey Owls in the Arctic. It was far outside the breeding season and we saw no birds there.

The second one was a true hollow going deep into the trunk of another big oak. Naturally, we were not expecting to see an owl there either and were totally unprepared for the sight of a Ural Owl looking out of the entrance. Whether or not this was just a roosting hole or an intended nest site was a question which we could not answer but the fish owls had used this hole last year and the Ural Owl would need to be on its' guard.

I spent both my last two evenings in the hide by the pool and the fish owls came both times, two birds on the first night and one on the second. There were not many nights of fishing left to them, for soon the pools and rivers would freeze and they would have to survive the winter by hunting small mammals and birds.

On the first night, it was the big female who was first to come and last to leave but she caught no fish. For an hour she stood motionless beside the water until the male came. By contrast, he waded out almost at once and within seconds had a fish, swallowed it and was gone. When he left, she began to fish too but struck twice and missed both times. The difficulties of catching a fish in the dark must be enormous and I am still uncertain of just how it is done. Perhaps it is the feet which finally sense the exact location of the fish for, after long periods of watching from the edge, the strike usually came almost immediately, once the owl had walked out into the water. I certainly had the impression that, although it was the watching which detected the presence of fish, there was some other technique which determined their precise location.

On my last night, I witnessed a lightning visit; the flight through the forest, then straight onto the log, into the water to seize the fish, swallow it and away, all in less than a minute. It might have been quick but it was as thrilling as ever, the final demonstration of the skills of a master fisherman, a sight which few people are ever privileged to see. We left Sumio and his owls with some sadness but with indelible memories of one of the most remarkable of all owls. It would be a major tragedy if this species was lost to the world.

OPPOSITE
Waiting in icy water –
Blakiston's Fish Owl.

Oregon

USA

Spotted Owl

I came to Oregon for one day to see the Spotted Owl. Even for an avowed fanatic, this sounds like a huge expenditure of effort and money for a very small return. In a way this is true but the Spotted Owl is a very special bird and it was a question of doing it this way or not at all.

The Spotted Owl is special in a number of ways.

Firstly, of all the owls that I have ever known, it has to take the prize for being the most confiding; so much so that some individuals seem to go out of their way to seek human company. Seen against the difficulties in obtaining even a glimpse of many owl species, this makes it an attraction in itself.

Secondly, the Spotted Owl is locked in the middle of a fascinating biological conflict, one which, sadly, it appears to be losing. Historically, the forests of the western seaboard of North America have been occupied by the Spotted Owl while those of the eastern side have been the home of the closely related but slightly larger Barred Owl. Now the Barred Owl is spreading its range westward and, in places, has reached Spotted Owl territory. Wherever this has happened, the Spotted Owls have simply disappeared. I know of no reports of direct conflict but it is clear that Spotted and Barred Owls cannot exist side by side and that it is always the Barred that prevails.

Why this is happening is unknown but it is certainly happening at a great pace. The first record of Barred Owls occupying new territory was in south-eastern British Columbia in the early 1960's. Since then, they have crossed the continent along the Canada-U.S.A. border and have moved north into south-eastern Alaska and south into Oregon and California. When a change occurs that is as sudden and as radical as this, it is tempting to conclude that some human disturbance must be behind it. Maybe this is so but there is no evidence and it is certainly too early to make that judgment.

The third factor which makes the Spotted Owl so special is that it is at the centre of a conservation battle which is so huge that it has attracted worldwide attention, not just in narrow biological circles but with the popular international media. There are many people around the world who have probably never seen an owl of any sort in the wild, yet who know about the conflict between loggers and conservationists over the Spotted Owl.

Spotted Owls are Wood Owls of the genus Strix and, more than any other species in the group, need old growth forest to survive. Their home is the ancient and magnificent coniferous forests of British Columbia, Washington State and Oregon, where Douglas Fir, Redwood and Hemlock grow to great heights. The forests are dense and the terrain where they grow is often steep but that is no problem to the modern logging industry, which, until recently, was clear-felling these forests at a speed which would have destroyed them all within a few years.

The danger to the Spotted Owl from logging has been recognised for a long time but reactions from government have varied. In Oregon, it was listed as threatened as long ago as 1955 and, in 1973, it was proposed that it be nationally listed as such. However, it took until 1990 for that listing to eventuate, a delay which resulted in vast areas of forest being destroyed.

The protection of many forests from further clearing caused the predictable uproar from the timber industry. It produced its own "research", claiming that, far from the owl being at risk, it was the timber workers who were the "endangered species" and that, if their activities were restricted, both the industry and the ten thousand jobs which went with it would be destroyed. The fact that they were rapidly clear-felling the forests, the owls and themselves to extinction seemed lost on them. Tempers have run high. Anti-owl bumper stickers have appeared on timber trucks and loggers have been known to remark that, if they saw a Spotted Owl, their first act would be to shoot it. Interestingly, an almost identical debate is being fought out in Australia with an uneconomical timber industry which sees itself as "endangered" and a threatened forest where owls and several species of marsupial have been publicised as examples of species at risk.

In this conflict, the Spotted Owls have become a symbol but it is far more than the owls' future which is at stake. The owls are just part of the intricate web of tree, plant, bird, animal, insect, fungus, bacteria, soil, water and climate which, over millions of years, have combined to make the majestic forests which, in remnant part, stand there today. They cannot be replaced. The timber industry can put in plantations and should do so but they are not replacing the forest. The plantation is a crop, no different in essence than a field of potatoes, planted to produce a yield and with no intent to recreate a fallen forest.

For a host of reasons, those forests should remain. Their complex, interdependent structure is at once diminished and altered if even one species is lost. They have a huge effect on climate, soil stability and water quality. They hold unknown chemical and pharmacological secrets which have yet to be researched. They are of huge interest to botanists, zoologists, naturalists, bird-watchers, hikers, artists and photographers. They are of an imposing splendour and a ravishing beauty, which is a tonic to the human spirit. It would be an act of unforgivable greed and selfishness if we destroyed them and left nothing for generations to come. We have no right to do this and they should remain.

OPPOSITE
The forests of Oregon, a patchwork of ancient trees and clear-felled re-growth

TOP
Eric Forsman, the world
expert on Spotted Owls.
BOTTOM
Spotted Owl among the ancient
mosses of an Oregon Forest

Our day with Eric Forsman was one of sheer delight. Eric is the great expert on Spotted Owls and it is his dedicated study over many years which has unveiled many of the birds' secrets and warned of the dangers. He met us in the town of Eugene, which lies in the valley between the Coast and Cascade Ranges, 50 miles in from the coast. We headed west, past marshes and lakes, then into the hills and towards the sea. It was mid-June, late spring and the whole countryside was green and lush.

Once we started to climb, we were into the forest and it was soon clear how much this had been changed by logging. There were large tracts of virgin forest but these were interlaced with plantations and with swathes of barren hillside where recent clear-felling had laid the ground bare. We climbed higher and eventually stopped along a narrow dirt road.

I found myself in a forest which was at once both immensely imposing and intensely beautiful. Douglas Firs were the dominant trees and they are huge, straight-trunked and anything up to 80 metres high or 250 feet to the locals here, where measurements remain in the imperial system. None of the trees were familiar to me but I was shown Hemlock and Cedar, lesser trees than the Douglas Firs but still huge. Inside the forest, the light was dim and the air still and cool. Festoons of green moss hung from the trees and coated their branches, soft ferns and fungi grew on the ground and, in the clearings, there were wildflowers; irises and a dwarf blue lupin, no doubt the ancestor of today's cultivated forms.

We made our way down a steep hillside, treacherously slippery underfoot. Unseen, a Winter Wren trilled from its hiding place and several trees carried the multiple drill holes of woodpeckers but, if there were other birds, they did not show themselves.

We were near the bottom of the hill when the male Spotted Owl called, a deep, four note hoot, rising for the middle notes and then falling back again. He was still some distance away, hidden among the trees but, even as I searched for him, I became aware of the female, quietly observing us from a perch less than ten metres away. Whether she had just arrived or had been there all the time I could not say but, if she had just flown in, she had done it very discreetly.

She was a sombre coloured bird, the archetypal wood owl, lacking the brilliant yellow eyes of the hawk owls or the dramatic ear tufts of the eagle owls. Her plumage was an almost uniform dark brown, peppered with the fine white spots which give the bird its name. Her big eyes were as dark as her feathers and she sat on a short, dead branch, close in to the tree trunk, so that it would have been very easy to pass her by.

TOP & BOTTOM
In broad daylight, a Spotted
Owl swoops through the
forest to snatch a mouse

1999 was not a good breeding year for Spotted Owls and this was one of the few pairs which seemed likely to be successful. It was mid-June. Spotted Owls lay early and, by now, it was quite likely that the young had left the nest. At nearly 200 feet in the broken-off top of a huge fir, it was not a site which was easy to examine. However, there were other ways to check on progress.

Eric had come prepared and put down a live mouse on the forest floor, almost at our feet. It was the first time he had done this since last season but the owl seemed to know what was coming, a sacrificial offering that was too tempting to refuse. The mouse was hardly out of Eric's grasp when the owl was on her way, snatching it with a sweep of the talons, which barely broke the rhythm of her flight, down across a gully and away into the forest.

Eric was expecting this. She was flying to the young and this was not the direction of the nest tree. He followed at breakneck speed, racing precariously across the ankle-breaking litter of the forest floor. He tracked her for nearly a quarter of a mile and, when we got there, he was looking up at two downy owlets, perched on adjacent branches about thirty feet above him. They were barely half the size of their mother and there was not a feather to be seen but, like the young of other Strix owls, they had left the nest long before they were able to fly, probably tumbling to the ground and then climbing back up to where we now found them.

The female was perched in a nearby tree, much lower than the owlets. There was no sign of the mouse and she must have taken that straight to the young. Eric produced another one. She was onto it in an instant, capturing it with the same fluid motion and carrying it straight up to the babies, where the lower one seized it and swallowed it head first.

Eric's protocol with the Spotted Owls was that, when they were offered mice, there were to be two for each owlet. Now it was time to try to band the young owls and the logic behind the protocol became clear. It was hard enough to catch an active baby owl and this was made infinitely more difficult and hazardous when under bombardment from an irate mother. However, with the promise of food, it could be possible to entice her out of sight.

Pete Loschl, Eric's co-worker, took the mice and walked away through the forest, showing them to the owl as he went. It worked and the owl followed him, giving Eric time to assemble his owl-catching tool. This comprised a thirty-foot pole with a slip-noose on the end, identical equipment to that used by the old Scottish wildfowlers to catch seabirds on the cliffs of the Hebrides. It seemed inconceivable that the owlet would stay there while Eric manoeuvred the noose over its head but, with skill born of many years' practice, he did and gently lowered the owlet to the ground. By now, the adult had realised that something was amiss and she returned but the job was done and, with the baby already on the ground, she did not attack. In minutes, the weighing, measuring and banding were done and the captive was ready to be released.

Young Spotted Owls may leave the nest before they can fly but they have an instinctive desire and ability to climb. There was a dead sapling, uprooted and sloping but checked from falling completely by its' head lodging in another tree forty feet up. We put the owlet there and at once, it started to climb. Within minutes, it reached the top and, from there, jumped and fluttered across to an upright, living tree where it made itself safe on the stump of a broken branch against the trunk.

The other owlet was out of reach, protected from the noose by a cluster of overhanging twigs. With a steep climb before us and another owl to visit, we needed to move on.

The walk in to the second owl was superb, through virgin forest, which had never seen an axe or a chainsaw. It was also even more precipitous than the first place and, by the time we reached the bottom, Eric was well in front. He had already found the owl or, I suspect, more correctly, it had found him, for these birds seem to have an innate curiosity where humans are concerned.

Seen apart, I could not differentiate Spotted Owl sexes but Eric assured me that this was the female. She was perched in a shrubby tree, which offered her some protection from the pair of Varied Thrushes, which were harassing her with much noise and vigour. Last year's nest tree was 200 yards away, another ancient Douglas Fir with a hollow where its crown had broken away. Nobody knew if it had been used this year.

Pete put down a mouse and she took it at once, just as the first bird had done. However, this was not to lead us to the young and she went back to the bushy tree where she stayed for some minutes with one foot on the prey. Then she picked it up and swallowed it. Perhaps food was scarce and she was very hungry herself. Pete put down another mouse, then a third and a fourth. She sailed down to grab each one and ate them all herself.

It was looking as though this pair had either failed or, perhaps, had not bred this year at all. However, Eric had walked away in search of the male and had found him. There was one mouse left and the male flew off with it, further downhill to where a single owlet sat on a fallen log. It was much smaller than the first two and seemed weak. We put it on a higher perch where it seemed content to stay, not trying to find itself a better spot as the earlier owlet had. Prey was hard to find this year and many of Eric's owls had abandoned their

TOP
Eric Forsman and Pete Loschl
measuring a young Spotted Owl.
BOTTOM
Fledgling Spotted Owl, already
out of the nest although still
a long way short of being able
to fly.

breeding attempts. It seemed that this pair too was at the very limit between success and failure.

It had been a long day and sunset was approaching when we emerged, panting, at the top of the hill. We were in a forest clearing and a repeated buzzing noise drew our attention to a Nighthawk, one of the North American nightjars, high above us and going through its spectacular display flight. With each call, we could see the white throat and open gape and then it would tip suddenly, wings thrashing as it went into a vertical dive which would not have disgraced a Peregrine. At the bottom of the dive it rocketed skywards again, changing direction as though it had bounced and, as it did, there came a loud tearing sound of tortured, vibrating feathers. The dive was repeated, over and over again and each time there was the same remarkable sound. I watched carefully and, at the bottom of the dive, the wings stopped beating and were held out sideways, stiff and bowed while the air tore at the flight feathers and the bird changed direction under a G-force which it would have taken an aeronautics expert to calculate.

It was time to go and we left with the Nighthawk still loudly and visibly advertising his territory. It had been a remarkable day and, if I were never to see another Spotted Owl, I was left with an indelible impression both of the bird and of the many problems and questions surrounding it.

Queensland

Australia

Lesser Sooty Owl

Rufous Owl

Lesser Sooty Owl

It was a night of that utter darkness which is so typical of the rain forest. Not a glimmer of light found its way to the ground and, as I looked up through the canopy, even the silhouettes of the treetops were gone, merged invisibly into the black of the night. The air was quite still and, as though hushed by this calmness of the elements, there was not a sound from any living creature. Almost inevitably, it was raining softly.

Then, with the piercing intensity of an electric shock, the call came; a spine-chilling downscale shriek, intensely shrill and penetrating, stopping me in my tracks and bringing a surging thrill of fear, even though I knew the source of the sound. This was the call of the Lesser Sooty Owl, the so-called "Bomb whistle". Whistle it may be when heard from a distance but this bird was right above me and the sound arrived as a blood-curdling scream, one of the most unearthly of all owl calls. It came once only and the silence returned as though it had never been broken. Moments before, I had been navigating my way through the forest by torch and this was the likely stimulus which had provoked the call, a common reaction by sooty owls of both species to the presence of artificial light.

The Lesser Sooty Owl belongs to the genus Tyto, an almost worldwide group whose best-known member is the cosmopolitan Barn Owl. Typically, Tyto owls are birds of open country but the two "sooties" have evolved far from this. The Lesser Sooty is the most specialised of all, superbly adapted to its life in the rainforest or, more specifically, in the north Queensland rainforest of Australia, for it occurs nowhere else in the world. Most Tytos hunt mainly by hearing and, to this end, have huge ears and, for owls, relatively small eyes. The Lesser Sooty also has the huge ears but, together with the closely related Sooty Owl, has the biggest eyes of all Tytos, a clear adaptation for navigating through the tangled blackness of its home.

Until recently, very little was known about the Lesser Sooty Owl and it was not until 1980 that it was recognised as a full species in its own right. Hardly any nests had ever been found and its dense, wet habitat had added an extra dimension of difficulty to the usual problems of studying a nocturnal bird. In the last twenty years there has been some excellent new fieldwork but it still remains true that almost any observations will reveal something about the bird that was previously unknown.

OPPOSITE
The mysterious Lesser Sooty Owl is confined to the rainforests of north-east Queensland.

I saw my first Lesser Sooty in 1985, a silvery shape in the headlights emerging out of the mist along a ridge-top track. I met three that night as they scanned the ground for prey from the overhanging branches of the Red Ash trees. With remarkable acceptance, one allowed me to walk almost beneath its perch, while I took multiple flash pictures.

That year was my first experience of the rainforest at night. It is a daunting environment. As well as being dark, it is steep and wet and slippery. The ground is littered with fallen trees and everywhere are the grasping, interwoven tendrils of the Lawyer Cane, reaching out to hook inexorably into every stitch of passing clothing, denying all further progress until they are painstakingly detached. It is also prime leech country and it takes only a few moments of standing still to trigger an assault from the waiting ranks. By day one may see the sinuous black forms looping across the forest floor, homing in like spokes coming to the hub of a wheel. After dark they just arrive, silently and painlessly, and the first inkling of their presence may be the blood-filled shoe and the blue, distended body of the leech, which drops from a sock at the end of the night.

Leeches are not the only parasites. There is the scrub-itch mite, the ubiquitous scourge of the north Queensland rainforest. Microscopic and unseen, they are present on every damp surface and clothes present no barrier to them at all. To sit on a mossy log is to invite trouble and they head straight for the warmest and moistest parts of the skin, there to set up an intense

RIGHT
Perched in the forest canopy, John Young waits and listens for the Lesser Sooty Owl.
FAR RIGHT
At the foot of the Lesser Sooty Owl tree. The nest hole is just above the projection on the left.

RIGHT
High in the rainforest, D.H.
looks across from the hide
to the Lesser Sooty Owls'
nest hole.
FOLLOWING PAGE
Arrival. A Lesser Sooty Owl
flies in to the nest with a
pygmy possum

irritation which can last for weeks. A night or two in this environment is usually all that it needs to become acutely aware of their invisible presence.

These are some of the problems of the rainforest at ground level. To find the Lesser Sooty Owl brings the added difficulty of needing to climb. Fortunately, I had as my ally John Young, Australia's greatest owl expert and a formidable climber. Without him, my study of Lesser Sooty Owls would not have gone far beyond hearing that first scream coming down to the forest floor.

I have been with John during many of those searches. It is not a task which can be carried out with any speed, nor indeed with any certainty at all. For this job, vision is useless and sound is the key to success; directional sound. On the ground, there is no hope of achieving this, for the calls, if they do reach there, are usually muffled and distorted, giving very little clue to their point of origin. The only place where the owls' voices take on any directional qualities is high up in the forest canopy. This is beyond the reach of my meagre climbing abilities and John went there alone. It needs great climbing skill, an intimate knowledge of owls, enormous dedication and a good slice of luck, for this is not only testing work. It is also very dangerous.

The night that John sat up in the crow's nest fern started well. The evening before, a Lesser Sooty had been calling very close by and, 25 metres above the ground, the uncluttered platform of the fern made a good listening post. At dusk, he climbed the tree that held the fern and settled in for a long wait. Sometimes the owls call early but others may be silent until long after dark.

The night was still and calm when, without warning, there was a crack and the tree beside the crow's nest fern began to drop away. To John, it seemed that it was his tree that was falling, just as a stationary train may seem to be moving when another one goes past the window. In that moment of uncertainty, he just hung on, convinced that his last moments had come and then the falling tree crashed to ground, sending tremors up the adjoining trunk to where John sat. He trembled too. It could so easily have been his tree.

1986 was the first year of serious searching and John found two nests, a remarkable feat of skill, perseverance and observation. Both were high up in huge Rose Gums, the only big eucalypts of the North Queensland rainforest. One hollow was at 30 metres and the other at a towering height of well over 40. John built tree hides to look across at both, balancing himself precariously in the tree-tops with hammer and nails, while I hauled up the building poles from the ground by rope and pulley.

It was an amazing exhibition of nerve and craftsmanship and later, with his help, I was able to make the climb up with camera and flash to spend several

nights there. We learned a great deal but it was impossible to site the hides close to the nest trees and the distances were too great for quality photography.

The following year, John went far beyond this, exceeding even his unique standards to find the extraordinary total of 17 active nests, all but one in an area of about 16 sq. km. of forest. This was considerably more than the total number of Lesser Sooty nests ever before recorded and required night after night of searching, often perched high in the canopy with hearing constantly attuned to note the exact bearing of a call. I doubt if anyone else in the world could have done it and John's success surprised even him.

Just what triggered such a breeding season remains a mystery. John has continued to search and to find the occasional nest but never any evidence of the explosion of breeding which took place that year.

My successes for that year were more modest. I learned much, took a few pictures and had a hide at one nest but my efforts were frustrated by soaking weather and then by a pair, which I had planned to photograph, having infertile eggs. A late starting pair seemed to offer some unexpected hope but abandoned the attempt even before the eggs were laid. I could not let matters rest there and determined that I would return one day and do the owls justice.

That chance came in 1991 with a pair of birds which seemed likely to be the same ones which had the infertile eggs four years before. They had moved about four hundred metres to a new nest tree, not far in open country but a huge distance in that dense forest and John's search for the new nest had been as testing as any he had done before.

We entered the forest and dropped downhill, following John's machete-hewn track to a small clearing, created by the fall of a great forest giant. At its edge stood the nest tree, a slender, bare trunk, 30 metres tall and without a branch below its crown. Its smooth, white bark was crusted with lichen and encircled by a high collar of crow's nest fern.

Half way up, the trunk widened around the opening of a large hollow, a smoothly rounded hole marking the site of some long-fallen limb. Here, weeks before, John had finally traced the owls to their new nest site. It was now late July and the female had been occupying the hollow for months. It seemed certain that she would have young.

Rainforest hide builders cannot be too choosy. The terrain rules out the use of towers while hides have to be built in whatever trees are available. Occasionally this gives an ideal site but very often it does not. This time, the hide, some fifteen metres above the ground, appeared to be supported entirely by a tangled mass of Lawyer Cane, which had bridged the gap between two saplings. Entry was gained by means of a walkway between two horizontal poles nailed to the trunk of one of the saplings. As I moved along it to the hide, the whole structure sagged disconcertingly but it was too late to be worried about that. I could only trust John's judgment and get on with the job in hand.

By 5.30pm, day was coming to an end and the sun was close to setting. It is a magical time of the day in the rainforest and, difficult country though it is, there are rewards in its extraordinary beauty. The late afternoon light glowed onto the canopy, enriching the forest greens with their infinite range of colour and texture. Then the sun was gone and the colours gradually deepened until they merged together in a uniform darkness with only the white trunk of the nest tree still glowing as though luminous.

Now it was still. The last White Cockatoos gave their final shrieks for the day leaving only a lone scrubfowl to continue crowing and cackling into the night. Then, from the hole six metres away, came the softest, fluting, rasping sounds. There was indeed a chick and it sounded to be still very small.

Ten minutes later the female began to call from in the hollow; loud, rasping noises that could easily have been mistaken for a Masked Owl. I had heard no sound from the male but clearly she had and I knew that he was on his way. A minute later there was a piercing trill from just to my left, so high as to be almost above human hearing. After a few moments, it came again and he was on the rim of the hole, a tiny Pygmy-possum dangling from his bill. He jumped down inside and there were screams from the female as he passed the prey. Then, within a minute, he was out and gone, flying quite silently into the night.

For nearly an hour, the female continued to rasp softly in the hollow but finally the sounds changed and I heard the choking, gurgling noises that always signify when a chick is being fed. For us, this was not going to be an all night session and, a little before midnight, we made our way down into the forest and home.

That was the first of eight consecutive sessions that we had in the hide, once staying all night but usually leaving before midnight. On five nights, the male arrived with prey within little more than an hour of sunset and, as with most owls, this was clearly the most profitable time for hunting.

On August 1st, he was there before 7-0pm, arriving quite silently with a rat in his bill. For a moment he paused at the entrance, a sooty black form dotted with silver, characteristically round-shouldered and with big, black eyes. Then he dropped down into the hollow amid throaty screams, which seemed to come from both birds. His stay was as short as the last one but then, ten minutes later, he was back in again with another animal and the sequence was repeated.

We waited in a silence that was broken only by crickets and tree-frogs. It

seemed unlikely that he would be back again but then, at 11.30pm, his high trills commenced just behind the hide. By now, John, who was filming the birds, had lights on the nest and the male was reluctant to come in. Repeatedly he trilled and the female rasped back from the hollow and then, from very close by, came the icy scream of a third Lesser Sooty.

At once, both parent birds became totally silent. Sensing problems, we dimmed the lights and it took only moments for the male to come in with the food. He came out even more quickly than usual and, at once flew into the crown of a nearby tree and began an intense trilling, loud, sustained and extremely musical. Within moments the female joined in and their calls filled the forest in a beautiful and very moving duet that went on for minutes. Moving though it may have been for me, the chorus had, of course a much more pragmatic function, a strong message of ownership that was directed straight at the third owl which had had the temerity to trespass on their territory.

On July 31st, we stayed all night. The male brought prey at 7.30pm and then followed the customary silence, broken only by the calls of two distant Boobooks, probably Red Boobooks for we were high up in mountain forest and that is their home. I fell asleep but was woken at midnight by the male sooty's screaming trill as he made another lightning visit with food. It was 5.0am before we heard him again, a loud bomb whistle that was very close. Perhaps he would have come in but John switched on the generator for his film lighting and that may have inhibited him. He called again just before dawn but, as the daylight returned, there was no sound from the female and the night's activities were over.

It is now nineteen years since I saw my first Lesser Sooty Owl. I have had hides at five nests and seen several more and yet I feel that I have hardly started. This fascinating wraith of the rainforest draws me back like a magnet and I can only hope that I shall have the chance again to be perched high in the canopy and hear the scalp-prickling call of the Lesser Sooty Owl.

Footnote 2004   Taxonomy is forever changing our concept of species, creating two where we had believed there was only one and merging what we had thought to be two back into one. Now it is happening to the Lesser Sooty Owl and, after 24 years as a distinct species, the scientists are now telling us that their DNA studies show that the Sooty and Lesser Sooty Owls are, after all, a single one. I am not a taxonomist so it is difficult to argue but I am only glad that I have been able to work on both birds, so clearly different in the field, and to fall under the spell of this fascinating little owl of the rainforest.

Rufous Owl

I was in the Rufous Owl hide on the night that the chick flew. It was a night to remember.

Any meeting with a Rufous Owl is an event. Rarest of the Australian mainland owls, it is also the most dramatic, a slightly smaller cousin of the Powerful Owl but with a very different temperament, particularly around the nest where it is always bold and often frankly belligerent. Its' home is the rainforests of northern Australia, particularly the gallery forests of lowland creeks but, despite its' boldness, it is quiet, cryptic and extremely hard to find. That I have seen eight active nests and been able to take photographs at half of them is a tribute to the skill and patience of John Young who found them all.

For the previous two nights, John and I had spent the first few hours of darkness there together and it was clear that the young owl was close to leaving. Standing in the rounded opening to the nest hollow, it tried repeatedly to use its' wings but was inhibited by the rim of an entrance which was too small to accommodate them. It was fed only once when the female accepted a part-plucked bird from her mate, flew with it to the hollow and tumbled down inside with the chick following her.

When the chick did fly, I was there alone for the whole night, with ample opportunity to take notes.

5.30pm I am sitting in an open-fronted hide, high in the canopy and looking out along a quite lovely rainforest creek. Eight metres away and directly in front of me stands a young Rufous Owl at the entrance to its' nest hollow, so near to flying that it may well leave tonight. Almost more beautiful than its' parents, it looks snow-white as it faces me; white breast, white belly and white trousers. The eyes are pale green with the face blackish, giving a spectacled appearance. There are brown feathers appearing in the crown and stiff bristles at the base of the bill.

The nest tree is a huge paperbark, its' trunk a somewhat dingy shade of white, everywhere flaking and peeling to reveal the warmer tones of the deeper bark below. All around, the long, slender leaves stream gracefully in the breeze. Beyond the nest tree, my eyes stretch on to the many shapes and colours of the rainforest trees; dark greens, pale greens, leaves that are shiny, leaves turning red, trees covered in blossom. How many species there are I have no idea but no two trees look the same. My eyes sweep on down the creek for as far as I can see, which is barely 200 metres, and then up the other side to where the male owl sits, guarding the nest from only 15 metres away. When I arrived, his atti- tude had been threatening, crown feathers raised and eyes glaring. Later, I had watched him panting in the hot sun, throat feathers pulsating, but now he sits peacefully, ever watchful but at ease.

For some days, the owlet has looked ready to go. Downy on the breast but well- feathered on the wings, it must be close to flying. It likes to stretch, reaching up to an amazingly full height but the shape of the hole gives little scope for wing exercises and that may hold it back for a while yet.

6.0pm Now the light is fading fast. The owlet has been at the entrance for over half an hour and is restless, leaning forward and looking towards the silent male, wanting to fly.

 6.10pm Action! It climbs out of the hole and up around the back of the tree, one foot still on the top of the rim but the other on the loose, slippery, vertical bark. There is no going back now but it will stay there for a few minutes yet.

 6.20pm It is away, whether by intent or sheer accident, I am not sure. With lit- tle wings flailing, it thrashes across the creek on an unsteady and descending course to an uncontrolled crash-landing in the outer foliage of another tree. In its' 20 metre flight, it has dropped nearly half that in height. For several min- utes it stays there, spreadeagled, before working its' way higher up the tree and flying again, losing more height but finding a more stable landing place in the crown of a palm. The male has not moved.

OPPOSITE
Fledgling Rufous Owl at dusk; restless and wanting to leave the nest.

6.50pm Suddenly the female is there, perched briefly beside the male before swooping down to the chick, exposed on its' palm crown. She seems to sweep it along with her and they both perch lower down, deep in cover.

6.55 Relieved of his guard duties, the male flies and is back within minutes. I cannot see if he has food but the female flies to him, there is a squeal and then she is back beside the chick who is trilling frantically. Gradually the noise subsides and both adults perch near the chick, murmuring deeply like Powerful Owls. Finally, at 7.40pm, the male flies.

8.0pm What an incredible place! There is stillness but not silence for life is all around me. From afar come the eerie cries and wails of the Stone Curlews, rising in mournful unison before dying slowly away. Much closer to me, the scrubfowl never really sleep and break the night with bursts of demonic cackling. There are fruit bats and the monotonous chopping calls of the Large-tailed Nightjars, all against an incessant background of insect noise. Now there are fireflies drifting by, their pulsing points of brilliant light stabbing the darkness like the navigation lights of a passing aeroplane.

8.10pm There is a Rufous Owl only 10 metres away, perched against the sky behind me. Cautiously, I swing the camera, point the flash, hope the focus is right and fire. Chances like this do not occur very often.

9.0pm An hour ago, I watched the moon rising behind the trees, two or three days past the full. Now it is high, bathing the earth in silver and dimming the light of the stars. Against the sky, the leaves make black patterns of feathers while the silhouettes of the branches are stark and sharp. In the distance, a Boobook is calling, melodious yet monotonous, the repetitive two note pattern its' only song.

11.30pm – 12.15am After a long period of silence, all the Rufous Owls are calling. First it was the female with soft, single "Hoo"s, interspersed with conversa-

OPPOSITE
Female Rufous Owl guarding
her newly-fledged owlet.

tional rumblings. This continues for half an hour until I realise that the male is there too, also giving single "Hoo"s. One bird flies up to perch near the hide, then down to the chick and away along the creek. The chick joins in with trilling too and probably it was fed but, in the darkness, many conclusions are only surmise.

12.30am – 4.30am   Even the owls are totally silent. Dawn and dusk are their most active times.

4.45am I can see no hint of dawn but a Lemon-breasted Flycatcher knows and starts singing, followed by a Buff-breasted Pitta and several Brush Cuckoos. The female Rufous Owl murmurs softly to the chick which trills in reply.

5.15am   Dawn is coming up fast. The Boobook is still calling but is drowned out now by the racket of kookaburras of both species.

5.40am Broad daylight. The owlet is perched in the foliage just below me. The Graceful Honeyeaters have just found it and are gathered all around, scolding. Bewildered, the baby owl peers up at them, trilling. Stiffly, I gather my gear and begin the long descent down the caving ladder to the ground.

I had been very fortunate. I had sat before at Rufous Owl nests but most of the action had gone on inside, hidden from my eyes. One night later and I would have looked out at an empty hollow. Later that day, we came back. The baby had not moved and the male was perched nearby, threatening. He did not attack but it would have been a different story after dark. Two days later, we returned for a final look but they had gone and we could not find them. The power of flight comes very quickly to a young Rufous Owl.

OPPOSITE, TOP
Journey's end. The baby owl's flight came to a halt in the crown of a palm tree.
OPPOSITE, BOTTOM
Soon after the owlet flew, both adults arrived to keep watch.

South Africa

White-Faced Scops Owl
Spotted Eagle Owl
Verreaux's Eagle Owl

P eter Steyn is southern Africa's owl man. He has seen every species, studied them, photographed them and written about them. I have been lucky to have him as a friend and as a guide on two African bird trips. The first time that I went, I hoped to see Pel's Fishing Owl. It eluded us and, by the next expedition, it had become our number one objective.

There was good reason for this for it is surely one of the most exciting of all the world's owls. It lives along the major waterways of southern Africa, particularly the Okavango River. It is a huge owl, in Africa second only to the Verreaux's or Giant Eagle Owl, with coppery plumage and big, black eyes. These features are dramatic in themselves but it is its' hunting methods which set it apart. At dusk, it leaves the seclusion of the riverine forests, flies to exposed perches above the water and watches. It is watching for fish and, when it spots one, it attacks with all the verve of a sea-eagle, gliding down to the river's surface to strike the fish from the water in full flight.

I dearly wanted to see this happen but it was not to be. We went to the Okavango and we did find the fishing owl but I had not counted on its extreme shyness, greater than I had experienced with any owl apart, perhaps, from the persecuted Eagle Owl of Austria. Twice we spotted a Pel's Fishing Owl high in a distant riverside tree and barely visible through the leafy canopy. That was as close as we ever came and, no sooner had we seen the owl than it too had seen us and was away.

A Botswanan guide took us to a small island with an old nest site, only five metres up in a big, open hollow. There were feathers on the ground, which were clearly from the owls but we were out of season and they were not breeding.

Unsuccessful by day, we cruised the backwaters at night, looking for hunting owls on their perches. It was fascinating work and we found roosting kingfishers, Carmine Bee-eaters and Little Bitterns but, if there were owls there, they eluded our eyes and Pel's Fishing Owl kept its secrets to itself. Fortunately, not every African owl was so uncooperative.

Until 1985, I had thought of all eagle owls as wary birds that kept away from man, inhabiting wild, remote spots or, at least, places which were hard to see and even harder to climb to. The Spotted Eagle Owls changed all that. They were nesting in a half-open hollow in a big, old pine, right beside the Cape Town ballet school. The window of the upstairs dance floor looked straight into the nest from only two metres away and the owls seemed quite unconcerned by the noise, the activity and, from time to time, the people who looked out at them.

OPPOSITE
At dusk, the male Spotted Eagle Owl arrived in the nest tree.

On the first day, I climbed to the nest to find the female barely half an arm's length away. The chicks were only a few days old and she had no intention of leaving, glaring at me with great, orange eyes and clacking her bill repeatedly. The male was close-by too, perched higher above me in the tree and I wondered if he would attack but nothing eventuated.

The following night, we watched at dusk from the ballet school window. Half obscured by the wall of the hollow, the female brooded the young and there was not a movement until half an hour after sunset. Then the male called from higher in the tree, a soft, triple hoot with a slight inflexion in the middle. The female stood, rearranged the young, made a soft croaking call and flew. She was away for fifteen minutes and returned quite silently.

It was another hour before I heard the male again. The female replied with her croaking call, continuing at ever-increasing tempo as I heard the male approaching. He landed with a big Brown Rat in his bill, passed it to his mate and was gone. We waited until ten o'clock but heard no more of him while the female took nearly an hour to finish the rat, giving tiny pieces to the two babies but eating most of it herself.

That was my only session but I was pleased to hear later that the young had grown up to fly. Long before that, we had headed north to the Kalahari Desert.

To Australian eyes, there is something very familiar about the Kalahari. Our road followed a dry river course between low sandhills, part-covered with dead grasses and small shrubs. It could have been the Strzelecki Track of northern South Australia but there were Acacias in place of Coolibahs and, despite the intense drought, they were bursting into bright green leaf. There seemed little there to sustain life but it was an illusion and the country held a large population of antelope, jackals, hyenas, lions and many species of birds. Among these was a pair of White-faced Scops Owls.

For most of the world's many species of scops owl, camouflage seems to be the imperative and their plumage reflects this, a cryptic mixture of muted blacks, greys and browns which can defeat the most searching eyes. The little White-faced Scops Owl is the exception.

They were nesting in the forked trunk of a thorny acacia, an open site and barely at head height. Just as with the Spotted Eagle Owls, the proximity of man clearly posed no barrier to them at all and it was almost as though they had chosen the site for this reason. There were African sleeping huts close to the tree and people walked repeatedly within metres of the nest. Perhaps the closeness of humans gave a protection against predators.

PREVIOUS PAGE
At dusk, the male Spotted Eagle Owl delivered a rat to the waiting female.
OPPOSITE
Two aspects of the White-Faced Scops Owl.
TOP
Seen from behind, relaxed with ear tufts lowered. The tail of a captured mouse is just visible below the branch.
BOTTOM
Alert with dilated pupils and the long ear tufts vertically erect.

I stood on a block of wood and found myself face to face with one of the prettiest owls I had ever seen. Less than a metre separated us as her orange-red eyes glowed at me from a big, white facial disc, made to seem even wider by its narrow black border. The bill was almost lost in a beard of white feathers and the overall plumage was silvery grey, finely streaked with black. Completing the picture were the two long ear tufts jutting out obliquely from the sides of the head. If she was afraid, she showed no sign and sat stock still, returning stare for stare.

I moved away and waited for the night. At 6.30 p.m., the sun set. Half an hour later, with the light almost gone, the owl sprang from the nest and disappeared into the darkness. She was away for only ten minutes, just long enough for me to check the nest and see that it held two eggs.

It was the drongos which told me that she was returning, Fork-tailed Drongos, which behaved just like the Spangled Drongos of Australia, scolding and mobbing her as she made her way back to the nest tree. She ignored them, landed near the top of the tree and then dropped down onto the eggs.

Half an hour later, the male arrived into a dead tree near the nest, silhouetted against the last glow of the evening sky. All detail had gone from the light but I could see his long ear tufts, now standing up vertically like two antennae, while the sinuous tail of a rat dangled from the perch below him. He called, a single low hoot, puffing out his throat feathers as the sound came. The female did not move.

Again he called and then again until, finally, after seven or eight hoots, she left the nest, landed beside him, seized the rat and flew on, leaving him to follow. For the next three hours, I saw nothing and heard nothing and began to worry that I might be keeping her off the nest. My fears were unfounded for, undetected by me, she had returned long before. As I walked away, I shone the torch to see the top of her head, the only part of her showing above the basin of the nest chamber, where she was bedded down deeply on the eggs.

Throughout all this activity, I had been standing near the nest with no hide or other form of concealment. With young in the nest, these owls would have been a brilliant pair to work on but safaris do not allow this sort of time and I had to move on.

Last among my African owls was the Verreaux's Eagle Owl, the largest owl in Africa and a bird of the woodlands. Its' size and power make it a formidable predator and, perhaps because of this, it seems to make no attempt to conceal itself. I saw several during my two African visits and all were in prominent spots, either perched in the open or sitting conspicuously on the old raptor nests which are its favourite choice for breeding. Sometimes the sight of a camera lens would cause an owl to squeeze itself low into the nest but that was about the only sign of concern that I ever saw in one.

Unfortunately, the ease of seeing Verreaux's Eagle Owl does not translate into ease of photographing it. Throughout the National Parks of southern Africa, there are strict rules which prohibit anyone from getting out of a vehicle or driving off a road. These are totally reasonable and understandable. Allowing vehicles to leave the road would lead quickly to great environmental damage and the logic that prohibits people leaving their vehicles is simple for, once outside, humans become just another prey species for the many large and often unseen predators.

Nevertheless, it was frustrating to have to view these seemingly unconcerned owls at a distance and through a tangle of branches when it was clear that just a short move into forbidden territory would give a clear view at a much closer range. It could not be.

Verreaux's Eagle Owl is generally a sombre greyish brown in colour but it has one strikingly prominent feature, obvious even from the distance that I was watching. The upper eyelids are a startling pink, made even more conspicuous by the bird's habit of drooping the lids. This hue seems scarcely natural, more like the work of an avant-garde beautician than a process of natural selection. Just what survival value it has remains a mystery. Peter Steyn has suggested that it is probably a feature used in display and that seems as likely an answer as any.

Peter has also remarked on the owl's ability to catch and skin hedgehogs, a skill which it shares with the Eagle Owl of Europe. In appearance, the two are the least similar of all the sixteen or so species of eagle owl but perhaps this habit points to a closer ancestry than is first apparent.

There is so much more to see and learn about the owls of Africa. I have long hoped to be able to return and spend more time with them but, as the security situation deteriorates through so much of the region, it is a hope which may never be realised.

OWLS Journeys around the world

OPPOSITE, TOP
The strikingly beautiful White-faced Scops Owl at her nest in a thorny acacia
OPPOSITE, BOTTOM
Verreaux's or Giant Eagle Owl. The name "Giant" is something of a misnomer for it is by no means the largest of the eagle owls.

Victoria

Australia

Powerful Owl

My journey with the Powerful Owl is more one of time than of distance. For nearly twenty years I have been trying to unravel its mysteries. I have spent countless hours walking the forests by day, listening for calls in the darkness and sitting in cold, cramped hides through the night. I have learned a lot but, measured against the effort expended, it is pathetically little. The Powerful Owl does not give away its secrets readily.

The Powerful Owl lives in the coastal forests of eastern Australia from central Queensland in the north to western Victoria in the south. It is the great owl of Australia, the world's biggest hawk owl, comparable in length, though not in weight, with the Eagle Owl of Europe, Verreaux's Owl of Africa and Blakiston's Fish Owl of Siberia, Manchuria and Japan. As well as being Australia's largest owl, it roosts in the open and needs large tree hollows to nest, all factors which should make it fairly easy to study. In fact, nothing could be further from the truth.

The problems begin with the country where the bird lives, mostly steep, hilly terrain with tall, dense forest, where the nest hollows may be thirty or more metres from the ground. Towards the extremities of its range, it does occur where the trees are smaller and the slopes gentler but, even here, any study is hampered by the owl's vast home range which may extend for kilometres through the forest.

Then there is the bird itself. The two best ways of detecting it are to hear it call or to find it at the roost. To hear a Powerful Owl call is to experience one of the great thrills of night-time in the Australian forest. The call of the male is a deep, measured "Wooo-hooo", rich in tone and far carrying. It is delivered all on one note and may be answered by the female whose second note is slightly higher than the first. Unfortunately, it is rarely used outside the first four months of the breeding season and, even then, some birds call very little. It takes a most dedicated owl fanatic to wait for hours in the cold of a winter's night in the possibly vain hope that a Powerful Owl may call from somewhere in the forest.

Finding roosts is a different proposition. At least this can be done by day but it is not easy. Powerful Owls like to spend the day free from mobbing by diurnal birds and, for their roosts, they choose places where there is deep shade and cover from above; under the canopies of Lilly Pillies, Casuarinas, Blackwoods and similar dense trees. Favoured roosts may be used for weeks or even months and then the telltale accumulation of whitewash and pellets begins to appear, one of the most useful of all clues for the owl watcher. These are not places which can be scanned from afar and a thorough search of an area requires an individual inspection of every possible roost site. Even then, the Powerful Owls often have the last laugh. Generally, they do not like to have their roosts discovered and I have lost count of the number of times I have painstakingly tracked down an occupied roost only for it to be abandoned the next night for a new and, for me, unknown resting place.

This then is the bird that has kept me guessing for all those years; the Powerful Owl, the enigma of the Australian forest.

To study the Powerful Owl, I chose to go to central Victoria. Here the forests of box and ironbark eucalypt are more open and considerably lower than in my home district of eastern Victoria. Here too, I had the help and friendship of three other owl men, Bill Flentje, Dale Gibbons and Rob Watkins.

Bill, in particular, was with me almost every time that I went. A retired forester, he has spent much of his life in Powerful Owl country. He is no longer a young man but his enthusiasm is boundless and we spent many nights in the forest in our quest for the owls. In particular, he is a highly expert wildlife sound recordist and his owl tapes have been invaluable in the field.

There were a few successes but many failures and frustrations. With many birds, I have been able to paint a very full picture of their lives from the study of one or two pairs. Not so with the Powerful Owls. Most seasons I learned a little bit more or managed to take a photograph or two but it was a painfully slow process, gradually pieced together with snippets of information from a number of pairs over many seasons.

The pair on Mount Alexander was the very first that I worked with and, in some ways, was the strangest pair of all. Throughout the twelve years that I knew them, the owls roosted in a ten hectare pine plantation, varying their choice of tree but rarely roosting outside the pines. This made them quite easy to find for, even when they were hidden in the crowns of the tallest trees, their whitewash and pellets showed up clearly on the carpet of fallen needles and ten hectares is not a big area to search.

These birds showed all the signs of being a virile and fertile pair. They had a very strong pair bond and often roosted together, they were always the earliest pair in the district to commence breeding and the male was by far the most aggressive Powerful Owl that I have ever met. With a picture like this, it was strange to find that their breeding record was one of almost constant failure.

I first met them in 1986 but Dale Gibbons had known them since 1978 and, from then until 1995, they were successful only twice in a total of eighteen breeding attempts. In 1996 the pines were felled, the owls disappeared and I have been unable to find them since.

1986 was one of the successful years. I came there in late May and found the birds among the pines, sitting close together in the same tree. From the amount of whitewash on the ground, they had been using the same spot for several days.

Sunset was at 5-0pm and I waited near the edge of the pines. Half an hour later came a deep "Wooo-hooo", the first evening call of the male. A few minutes later it came again but from a slightly different angle and then again, each call on a slightly different bearing from the one before as he moved towards the edge of the plantation. He emerged not far from me and perched on a bare limb, clearly silhouetted against the sky. He had no need of a silhouette to spot me and flew over my head, putting in a half-hearted sort of stoop. I thought nothing of it but it was a foretaste of things to come.

Now the female was also out of the pines and, a few minutes later, I heard the rabbit-like squeal, which she often gives at the moment of copulation. We tried to follow them but they had stopped calling and we lost track.

It seemed that our night's owling was over and, with the autumn air cooling, we lit a fire and boiled the billy. An hour later we were still standing over the coals when the two owls glided overhead together, silently, their outlines etched sharply against the silvered clouds of a high moon. Their course was set down the mountain and into the valley of a long, shallow gully. It took another eight weeks to find the nest there but, eventually, Dale traced it to a hollow in a Manna Gum, over a kilometre from the pine plantation.

This turned out to be a successful breeding season but there were other reasons too which made it notable. Unlike its near relative the Rufous Owl,

the Powerful Owl was always said to be timid around the nest and there were no records of it ever attacking people. It was with this knowledge that, in mid-August, Dale went at dusk to watch the nest. He sat a hundred metres away at the base of a tree and, as darkness fell, the male began to call and then flew in to land high in the nest tree. He had no food but, at his arrival, the female came out of the hollow and flew away. The male then dropped down to peer in the hollow but, shortly afterwards, the female returned and he retired to a nearby tree while she went back inside.

At this point, Dale judged that there would be no more activity for a while and stood up to leave. Possibly the male owl had failed to notice him until then for his reaction was immediate. He left his perch and came straight at Dale who hardly had time to cover his head before he was struck a shuddering blow on the shoulder. A big male Powerful Owl may weigh two kilogrammes and, with murderous talons, is a fearsome adversary. Dale was quite unprepared for the onslaught and was hit repeatedly by a bird, which continued its' attacks until he was several hundred metres from the nest tree. It was a salutary experience and we were all much more careful with our protective gear from then on. This owl went on to attack Rob Watkins and to terrorise Bill Flentje's wife when she was over a kilometre from the nest, sending her into hiding behind a tree until Bill returned to save the situation. In subsequent seasons, I too felt the force of his talons on my back and have come to treat all nesting Powerful Owls with great respect.

Why this pair of owls had such a poor breeding record is still a mystery. They had reared a chick in 1981 but, after 1986, had ten successive failures. A few bush walkers and trail hikers used the mountain but, overall, disturbance was very slight. Usually they failed at the incubation stage, sometimes even before we had found the nest, and they then might go on to try again in a new site but always with the same result. There were other pairs too which had only moderate success but the Mount Alexander birds were by far the worst. Eggshell thinning could have been the answer but no eggs were ever collected for measuring. Fortunately there were other birds which fared much better.

Since 1991, I have devoted my efforts to two pairs of owls, both in the forests to the south of Bendigo, the Bridge Pair and the Track Pair. At one time the forests here stretched unbroken over a vast expanse but now they are cut up into areas of a few hundred to a few thousand hectares, separated from each other by extensive belts of grazing land. This appears to be causing the owls problems with hunting and possibly also with the recruitment of new breeding partners.

Between 1991 and 1994, the Bridge Pair bred successfully three times. As

Powerful Owls go, they were an excellent pair to study, not aggressive, tolerant of my tower at night and, with a careful approach on my part, not too shy by day. Nearly always, they roosted under the canopy of big Cootamundra Wattles in a long shallow gully, often with the previous night's prey clamped below one foot, trademark behaviour of the two big Ninox owls. In mid-June 1992, the female disappeared from the gully and we knew it was time to look for the nest.

The previous year they had raised an owlet in a low, half-open hollow, less then five metres from the ground and two kilometres north of the roost gully. It was a vulnerable spot and it was no surprise that they had gone elsewhere for the next season. But where? A thousand hectares is not a big area as forests go but it takes a lot of searching. In early July, the male also stopped roosting in the wattle gully and we seemed no closer. Then, on a night in mid-July, I thought I heard a distant call far away to the south-west of the gully. It was raining and windy and not a night to be walking the forest but Bill and Dale went back a few days later and found the nest hole, fourteen metres high in the trunk of a Red Box tree. It was over three kilometres from the previous year's site.

This was to be a successful season and the young owl left the nest in late September. Female Powerful Owls do not occupy the nest hollow until they are ready to lay and when, the next year, she went in on June 5th, it seemed that all would be well again. Then, three weeks later, she was back with the male in the wattle gully and the nest appeared deserted. However, both birds continued to frequent the nest tree area and, towards the end of July, she was back in the hollow again. It was not to be. Possibly this second attempt was too late in the year but, at the end of August, the site was abandoned for the second time.

Whatever the cause of that season's problems, the owls remained faithful to the site and, in 1994, made up for the earlier failure by fledging two young. This was a marvellous pair to work with. The male was particularly approachable and, when he was roosting in the wattle gully, would let me creep up within portrait distance with the 600mm lens, watchful but seemingly not too concerned if I moved slowly. Characteristically, he often held the previous night's prey, draped across a branch and clamped beneath one foot. Usually it was a Ring-tailed Possum and the slaughter of this species where Powerful Owls occur is colossal.

The female was no less obliging. This time, I put up my tower at the nest, 12 metres back and with the hide eventually level with the entrance. She accepted it without hesitation and took very little notice of the intermittent bursts of light from the flashes when she came to the nest. Tree hollows have a limited span of usefulness and, before the next season, the entrance of the

hollow collapsed. By this time too, the female had disappeared. Probably she was dead for it seems certain that the strongly residential Powerful Owl mates for life. She was not replaced and the male stayed on alone until, four years later, he too disappeared. That territory is now unoccupied.

We had seen owls in the region of the Track site for some years but it took until 1995 to find what appeared to be the nest tree, too late for that season but with all the signs of recently completed breeding. Confirmation came the next year and the same hollow was used successfully for the next four years, twice fledging two young. Then, in 2000, the female of this pair also went missing and the male was left in the forest alone, still calling when it was well into the breeding season and clearly looking for a mate who had failed to appear. It always seemed possible that a new female would arrive but I had watched events like this several times before and the signs were ominous. For a year, the male still frequented his favourite roost sites but then he too vanished and has not returned.

Of all the Powerful Owls that I worked with, I came to know this pair best of all. A friend first saw them in 1991 and suspected that they were breeding but, until 1995, I could find them only intermittently. Then, in April 1996, we found both birds roosting in a grove of Red Box trees. From the mess of whitewash and pellets below the trees, they had been perching there for some time. This was only 300 metres from the suspected nest tree of 1991 and 1995 and was a highly promising lead.

Confirmation came two months later when I returned with Bill. Now the focus of droppings had shifted to the ground beneath a dead ironbark close to an old Grey Box and it seemed certain that the box was the nest tree. There was no sign of the female but there was a big dead spout coming off the tree with a large entrance hollow and she was surely inside. Fifty metres away, the male was perched high in another Red Box, a Brush-tailed Possum beneath one foot.

We waited at dusk. At five o'clock the sun set but it was another half hour before the male uttered a soft "Wooo-hooo". Silence followed and he waited ten minutes before calling three times more. Now there came a soft answering "Woo-hoo" from within the hollow, followed by the sound of scraping talons as she came up to the entrance. She flew to a nearby branch, paused and flew again. The male must have followed her and both birds began calling from further up the hill. To stay longer would only put stress on them and we slipped quietly away.

In a Powerful Owl's nesting cycle, I find it useful to divide the time into three phases. The first is incubation and lasts for about 38 days from when the female first enters the hollow. After hatching comes the period of constant

OPPOSITE
1997 The Track. Pair of Powerful Owls roosting together. Female on left of picture. With young well over a month old, she no longer broods them by day.

brooding when she leaves the nest only to take food from the male or for very brief periods of respite. The third phase begins when the young are about a month old and the female ceases to brood by day, although she may still return to the hollow for longer or shorter periods at night.

From a photographer's point of view, these phases have a vital importance. During incubation, the Powerful Owl is very susceptible to disturbance, may readily abandon the eggs and it is best to stay right away. The same applies in the second phase although for a different reason. Nesting takes place in the middle of winter and the female, once disturbed by day, will almost certainly not return until night, when the young may already have succumbed from cold. It is only during the third phase that it is safe to create the inevitable disturbance around the nest. By this time the young are big enough to maintain their body temperature alone and the female's attachment to the nest is at its strongest.

For nine weeks we left the owls to themselves and it was August 16th when we returned. Our timing was right and the female was out of the nest, perched at the same height in another tree only ten metres away. I had a good team with me and, in less than an hour, we had the tower up, twelve metres back from the nest tree and still only at half height. Throughout our activities, the female stayed and watched us and she had still not moved when we finally drove away.

The next evening was wet. We lifted the tower to its full height and left the owls to get accustomed to it. The following afternoon I climbed to the hide for my first session. It was cold. To the west in Adelaide there had been snow the day before and it felt to be coming ever closer.

It always takes time to get organised for the first session and the sun had already set before I was ready. Outside, the Fuscous Honeyeaters had discovered the occupied hollow and were gathered in a frenzy of excitement around the entrance, shouting abuse at the occupant and then, like children, darting away before the young owl could react. It was all false bravado, for the owlet would be nest-bound and helpless for some weeks yet, but it was a ritual which I have seen many times involving owls of several species. White-plumed Honeyeaters do it and, in Queensland, Yellow Honeyeaters behave in exactly the same way with Rufous Owls. For the owl watcher, it serves the very useful purpose of confirming that a hollow is occupied.

Footsteps sounded below the hide but they were not human and I looked down as a troop of kangaroos thumped past the base of the tower, oblivious to my presence just above them. Then, faintly, came the shivering trills of the young Powerful Owl in the nest. Not all the sounds seemed to be quite at the same pitch and I wondered if there were two young.

OPPOSITE
1999 The Track. With a Ring-tailed Possum in her bill, the female arrives back at the nest

It was still half light when I realised that the female had arrived. From just behind me came the strange, nasal, pulsing murmur which, in varying forms, is a call which is used only around the nest. Sometimes, as at this time, it is a conversational call to the young, soft and intimate. Sometimes it is a sign of anxiety and then the throb and the volume both increase. At its peak, it is a sign of anger or alarm when it becomes a loud, sheep-like braying though still retaining its nasal quality. In the darkness of the night, it has a disturbingly eerie effect.

She had come in quite silently, remarkably so for such a big bird, and in marked contrast to other occasions when she would crash through the foliage onto her perch. I wondered if these crash landings might be quite deliberate when she wanted to advertise her presence.

Her murmuring became more animated and I thought she would fly to the nest but then I heard the voice of the male a little further away, deeper but otherwise very similar. For a minute more they conversed with each other, the murmurings becoming more urgent until I heard her fly towards him, there came the rabbit-like squeal and, a moment later, she was tumbling into the nest hollow.

She stayed inside for only a minute and, when she flew, the murmurings began again from both birds. Three times came the squeal and then, when she flew to the nest again, there was still just light enough for me to see that she had a Ring-tailed Possum in her talons. This time I fired the flash and she did not like it, flying off with the prey. Again the murmurings began, not yet the full bleating of alarm but they were distinctly uneasy. I sat rock still and silent while calm gradually returned. Eventually the sounds died away and, half an hour later, she came to the nest quite silently. This time I held my fire and she went quickly inside. The trilling stopped and was replaced by the cracking of bones and the half-strangled noises of a young owl choking down pieces of meat which were almost too big for it.

Half an hour later, the female emerged and flew but not far, going to her favourite perch near my hide where she continued to murmur softly from time to time. She was still there when Bill came to see me out of the hide at ten o'clock.

The next night, I had two long, cold spells in the hide, going in from mid-afternoon until 10-0pm and again from 3-0am until after dawn but they were fruitless vigils. For most of the time, the female was perched close behind me but she did not come to the hole. Occasionally the young trilled and she talked back quietly in return, quite calm and unconcerned. With no food, she had no reason to visit. Soon after 6.0am, the morning chorus began and it was more than half light when, half an hour later, the male returned. Close by the hide, he filled the forest with over thirty loud double hoots before his voice

OPPOSITE
1997 The Track. Young
Powerful Owl, almost ready to
leave the nest

seemed to go hoarse and he stopped. I doubt if he had food and there was no reply from the female.

When it was fully light I came down from the hide. On our track behind the tower lay a tiny dead Sugar Glider, only five centimetres long. It had not been there the evening before and must have fallen from its mother's pouch when she was brought to the nest as food. Clearly there had been action during my five-hour absence from the hide.

Two hours later I had the tower down and was driving out of the forest. I had run out of time but Bill kept a watch on the nest and confirmed our suspicion that there were two young. They flew in mid-September but it was late October before I had a chance to return to see them. They were still with their parents, roosting all together in the grove of Red Box where we had first found the adults. Unlike the old birds, they were nervous and jumpy, watching us with staring eyes until they exploded out of the tree, taking their parents with them. They scattered in all directions and there seemed no point in pursuing them.

For five consecutive years this pair returned to nest in the same hollow and, for the last four, I returned with them, following their fortunes both from the ground and from my hide at the top of the tower. It was a fascinating experience and, though much of what they did was repetitive and predictable, I was continually being surprised by something new.

Many features were the same each year. Always it began with their return to the Red Box grove to roost. Then, as they began to visit the hollow at night, the whitewash would start to appear near the nest tree. This was among their most secretive times and, despite all the evidence there, I never witnessed one of those pre-laying visits. Once the female was incubating, the male started to move his roost nearer the nest tree, often coming progressively closer until he was a bare thirty metres away. More often than not, there was prey clamped below one foot. Most of his success seemed to come late in the night and invariably he held onto this until the next evening, possibly eating the head before dawn but never anything during the hours of daylight.

Ring-tailed Possums were by far the commonest prey and he took a fearful toll of them but there were birds too, particularly Galahs but also White Cockatoos, Australian Magpies, Pied Currawongs and Australian Ravens. Less common prey was the large Brush-tailed Possum but I never recorded this bird catching the introduced and common Rabbit.

The reasons for the pre-dawn hunting are not hard to deduce. Powerful Owls hunt much more by sight than by hearing, and even with their acute night vision, they need the faint light of dusk and dawn to succeed. They take large prey which, of necessity, is usually widely dispersed, and so the Powerful Owl must disperse too, covering a huge area of country in its search for food. Just how huge is this area was discovered in 1999 when Todd Soderquist, a wildlife researcher, managed to trap the male and attach a radio transmitter. Subsequent monitoring showed the owl ranging far beyond the confines of the forest, out into open farmland and along distant strips of roadside trees. His forays took in an area of over 3000 hectares and, with such distances to travel, it was quite obvious why early evening hunting success was the exception.

Just as the dawn arrival with prey was the norm, so was the evening feed for the young. At dusk the female always moved close to the nest, replying softly to the young birds' eager trilling. If the male had food, he would soon pass it to the female, by which time larger young were in a frenzy of anticipation, white heads seeming to glow in the dark as they scrambled up into the entrance of the hollow.

These were some of the predictable happenings but others came as a total surprise. On August 31st 1997, the owlet was within a week of flying. Bill and I arrived in mid-afternoon and soon found both adults. He had no prey but, surprisingly, she had a Ring-tailed possum, the first time that I had seen her with prey by day. At dusk, she moved to her usual tree behind my hide. I waited for her to come in but, when she flew, she went straight past the nest hole and onto a dead limb higher in the tree and silhouetted against the sky from where I sat. The young owl could see her too and was frantic with anticipation, trilling constantly and standing up in the nest entrance, swaying from side to side.

What followed was totally unexpected when the male flew up to land beside her and she began to feed him, pulling off little morsels from the possum and passing them bill to bill as though feeding a tiny chick. Altogether she passed him fifteen small pieces and then, when he flew, she followed him and there was a burst of intense squealing behind me, which seemed to come from both birds. Then the whole performance was repeated with the female once more flying up to the dead limb and feeding the male who had followed her. Again he flew first and, when she followed, there was more squealing behind the hide before I heard the sound of his departing wings. Only then did she come to the hole and by this time it was too dark for me to see if she brought the prey with her. Certainly there were no sounds of feeding and it seems possible that the male left with the food himself. Five days later, the young bird was almost ready to leave and Bill found both adults with prey, the male with a young Brush-tailed Possum and the female with a Ring-tailed.

This surely meant that both adults were hunting and could be the explanation for what I had seen from the hide a few days before. That night, the female may have been the only successful hunter.

The attack on my flash units was a less natural event but no less unexpected. It was late August 1998 and I had already had three nights in the hide and taken a few pictures. To avoid the problem of "Red eye", the big Metz flash units were set out on steel rods, over a metre from the hide on each side.

Returning to the tower in the morning, my initial thought was "Vandals"! One flash unit was swivelled upside down while the other one, complete with two metres of steel rod, was hanging half way down the tower, knocked out of its socket but hanging on precariously by its electric lead. Fifteen metres from the base of the tower, the power cable to the flash battery lay on the ground.

Over many years, I have always found it quite safe to leave my tower standing, for very few people will risk climbing it. Certainly there were no signs of interference at ground level and, when I climbed to the hide, it was quite clear that nobody had been there since I left.

It had been a calm, windless night and there could be only one explanation; the owls themselves! They might have seemed accepting of my flashes but they did not like them and had set out to deal with them in the only way that they knew. I had come to think of this pair as non-aggressive but it seems that I was wrong and it had taken some fierce blows to cause that amount of damage. It is never wise to take Powerful Owls for granted.

Now it seems that this pair has gone. Fortunately, my last season in 1999 had been the best of all photographically but I was saddened to see another breeding pair seemingly lost. The female disappeared first while the male stayed on. For a while, I hoped that he might find another female but, in this region of fragmented forests, recruitment of new breeding birds does not always happen. I know of three other breeding territories in the district which are now unoccupied and there must surely be others.

It is hard to know what can be done to reverse the trend. Nest boxes might help, for some forests certainly have a shortage of large hollows but isolation of the owls plus prey shortage may be just as important. Many of these owls are now the sole occupants of patches of remnant forest far smaller than the 3000 hectares identified by the radio tracking. Too small to support more than one pair, their isolation may be a great barrier to the recruitment of new birds when one of a pair dies. Whatever the answer, there is clearly a problem which is crying out for an answer. I would hate to see the day arrive when the Powerful Owls of central Victoria had disappeared for ever.

OPPOSITE
1992. The Daytime Roost.
Male Powerful Owl in dense
cover; a typical site.

The Future

I have had a wonderfully fortunate time among owls with fascinating experiences all around the world. Inevitably, the question has come to me, "Will they still be there in the future? Will generations to come still be able to experience the thrill of these most mysterious of all birds?" It is a question which goes far beyond owls for they are a mirror to the state of the whole world environment.

In my mind, I took a trip through all the owl places that I had visited, trying to predict what might happen in the years to come.

In the far north, the Snowy Owls of the Arctic might seem to have an assured future. Few people visit their icy homeland and the lemmings, which the owls hunt, pose no threat to human interest. However, despite the reverence which the native peoples have for the bird, they still shoot it and, in recent years, an unwelcome habit has arisen of taking chicks from the nest to keep as pets. However, these problems are trivial compared with the recent news that the United States government's will lift its' ban on oil exploration and extraction in the great Alaskan wilderness, a decision which is hardly a surprise but which is not good news for any of the wildlife of this almost untouched region. Finally, above all this, hangs the prospect of global warming which could have particularly profound effects on the fragile environment of the Arctic.

With the Spotted Owls of Oregon, the threats are more obvious and immediate. Logging of old forests has already wrought great harm and, although slowed, it has certainly not stopped. Added to this, there is the retreat of the Spotted Owl before the advancing Barred Owl, a phenomenon which may or may not have been induced by man but which is bringing no good at all to the Spotted Owl's future.

In Costa Rica, the greatest threat to the Spectacled Owl seems to be forest clearance. At present, there still appears to be ample forest remaining and the government has a commitment to conservation but the same may not apply in other parts of the tropical Americas.

In Argentina, the Burrowing Owl has certainly suffered around the cities but the country is huge with a sparse human population so all would seem to be well. The same species in southern U.S.A. has not been so fortunate where an explosion of people has claimed huge areas of its' grasslands for farming, housing, golf courses and other human needs.

OPPOSITE
This young Eagle Owl has already left the nest, making its' future a little more secure but the species is still persecuted in some countries.

Across the Atlantic, the Barn Owls of Britain have had a hard time and, in the fifty years to 1985, the population in most districts has been shown to have fallen by an average of 75%. Hunting habitats have been reduced with the bulldozing of hedges and the loss of rough grassland. This habitat loss has affected prey numbers too and then, with the use of persistent rodenticides, some prey animals have become living doses of poison for the owls. On top of this, hollow nest trees have fallen with age or been cut down and many old owl barns have been converted into modern houses with no provision for owls to live there. On the positive side, the British have a great tradition for wildlife conservation and the many people working to protect owls have certainly helped to stem the problem so that the British Barn Owl appears now to be slightly on the increase.

In Finland, there is no lack of forest or of prey. The problem is the shortage of nest sites and has been overcome with a prodigious number of nest boxes, put up and maintained by a small number of dedicated volunteers. There lies the risk! Finnish Ural and Tawny Owls are now almost entirely dependent on nest boxes and one can only hope that the tradition of nest box maintenance will be carried on by future owl enthusiasts.

Hunters are a threat to Austrian Eagle Owls. The same probably applies in other European countries but, in Austria, the effect has been profound, limiting the increase which had begun in the hunter-free years of World War II.

It is hard to know what is happening to African owls. Many Africans regard them as creatures of ill omen and will destroy them if the chance occurs but the numbers involved are probably small. Beyond that, my own experience is too limited to put forward an opinion.

The Christmas Island Hawk Owl is undoubtedly one of the world's most endangered owls. Unique to the tiny island, its' habitat had already been reduced by forest clearance for phosphate mining. Now, together with every other plant and animal on the island, it is mortally threatened by the advance of the Yellow Crazy Ant, the voracious invader from Africa which is destroying everything in its' path. Efforts are being made to exterminate the ants but it is a daunting task and the history of failed attempts in other parts of the world does not augur well.

For Blakiston's Fish Owl, the prospects in Japan are shaky. Thirty years of dedication by Sumio Yamamoto has quadrupled the population but it still stands at only 130 and Sumio will not be there for ever. If human help is ever withdrawn, 130 may not be a self-sustaining population but, even if help continues, the scarceness of good habitat makes it hard to see how the population can grow much more.

In Australia, there are environmental concerns aplenty but none that obviously threaten the overall survival of any of the owls. With the Powerful Owl, excessive forest clearing appears to be the cause of a marked decline in central Victoria but they seem secure in the big forests of the Great Dividing Range. Open country owls like the Barn, Masked and Grass have certainly all suffered from habitat clearance and from rodenticides, which could also have poisoned an occasional Lesser Sooty Owl, but this is primarily a bird of mountain rainforest and virtually the whole of its range has been protected by being proclaimed a World Heritage Area. So long as future governments honour this, it should remain safe.

The future of the Australian Rufous Owl seems less certain. Like the Lesser Sooty, it is a rainforest bird but its' preference is for lowland forest, a habitat which has been considerably reduced by land clearing. Not only has its' living space been reduced but now, with crops growing right to the forest edge, any owl which ventures outside to hunt may be at risk from agricultural poisons. In 1994, a North Queensland pair both died in the same week from the effects of rodenticide. Their fate only came to light because they were birds which John Young had been visiting regularly but there must surely have been more.

For me, this exercise in owl prognosis has been a telling one. There is scarcely an owl on my list whose outlook has not been profoundly changed in my lifetime, usually for the worse and because of human activity. Owls are my special interest but the same sort of prospects could be given for countless other animals, plants and other forms of life. When one considers that all of these species have been in existence for millions of years, it gives a measure of man's effect on the planet in recent times. If my survey had been carried out a hundred years ago, a thousand years or even longer, I suspect that the answer would have been. "All well! No change in status." What the answer will be in another fifty years is unknown but the signs are not good.

I can only be happy in the experiences that I have had and hope that others may get some vicarious pleasure through this book.

Further Reading

BRANDT, Thomas 1994 *Die Schleiereule* AULA Verlag Gmbh, Wiesbaden (*Text in German*)

BUNN, D.S., WARBURTON, A.B. and WILSON, R.D.S. 1982 *The Barn Owl* T.& A.D.Poyser, Calton, Staffs, England

BURTON, John A. 1992 *Owls of the World 3rd ed.* Peter Lowe Eurobook, London

CENZATO, Elena and SANTOPIETRO, Fabio 1991 *Owls Art Legend History* Bulfinch Press, Boston

CRAIGHEAD, John J.and CRAIGHEAD, Frank C.Jr 1969 *Hawks,Owls and Wildlife* Dover Publications, New York

DUNCAN, James 2003 *Owls Of the World* Key Porter Books, Ontario

FLEAY, David 1968 *Nightwatchmen of Bush and Plain* Jacaranda Press, Brisbane

HELO, Pekka 1984 *Yön Linnut – Kirja Suomen Pöllöistä* Kainuun Sanomain Kirjapaino Oy, Finland (*Text in Finnish*)

HOLLANDS, David 1991 *Birds of the Night – Owls Frogmouths and Nightjars of Australia* Reed Books, Balgowlah, N.S.W.

HOSKING, Eric 1982 *Eric Hosking's Owls* Pelham Books, London

HOSKING, Eric and NEWBERRY, Cyril 1945 *Birds of the Night* Collins, London

HUME, Rob and BOYER, Trevor 1991 *Owls of the World* Dragon's World, Surrey, England

JOHNSGARD, Paul A. 1988 *North American Owls* Smithsonian Institute, Washington

KEMP, Alan and CALBURN, Simon 1987 *The Owls of Southern Africa* Struik Winchester, Cape Town

KÖNIG, Claus, WEICK, Friedhelm and BECKING, Jan-Hendrik 1999 *Owls* Pica Press, East Sussex

MIKKOLA, Heimo 1983 *Owls of Europe* T.& A.D.Poyser, Calton, Staffs, England

NERO, Robert W. 1980 *The Great Gray Owl* Smithsonian Institute, Washington

NEWTON, Ian, KAVANAGH, Rodney, OLSEN, Jerry and TAYLOR, Ian 2002 *Ecology and Conservation of Owls* CSIRO Publishing, Collingwood, Australia

NORMAN, Janette A. CHRISTIDIS, Les, WESTERMAN, Mike and HILL, F.A.Richard 1998 *'Molecular data confirms the species status of the Christmas Island Hawk-Owl Ninox natalis'* Emu 98:197

NORMAN, J.A., CHRISTIDIS, L., JOSEPH, L., SLIKAS, B., and ALPERS, D., 2002 *'Unravelling a biogeo graphical knot: the "leapfrog" distribution pattern of Australo-Papuan sooty owls (Strigiformes) and logrunners (Passeriformes).* Proc. R. Soc. Lond. *B269: 2127-2133*

READ, Mike and ALLSOP, Jake 1994 *The Barn Owl* Cassell Plc, London

SAUROLA, Pertti 1995 *Suomen Pöllöt* Kirjayhtymä Oy, Helsinki (*Text in Finnish*)

SCOTT, Derick 1997 *The Long-eared Owl* The Hawk and Owl Trust, London

SHAWYER, Colin 1987 *The Barn Owl in the British Isles* The Hawk Trust, London

SPARKS, John and SOPER, Tony 1989 *Owls 2nd ed.* David and Charles, Devon, England

STERRY, Paul 1995 *Owls- A Portrait of the Animal World* Todtri Productions, New York

STEYN, Peter 1984 *A Delight of Owls* David Philip, Cape Town

SURMAN,Chris 2003 *Crazy Crisis for Christmas* Nature Australia 27/11:60

TAYLOR, Ian 1989 *The Barn Owl* Aylesbury

VALLÉE Jean-Louis 1999 *La Chouette Effraie* Delachaux et Niestlé. Lausanne (*Text in French*)

VOOUS, Karel H. 1988 *Owls of the Northern Hemisphere* William Collins, London

WALKER, Lewis Wayne 1974 *The Book of Owls* Alfred A. Knopf, New York

WEINSTEIN, Krystina 1985 *The Owl in Art, Myth and Legend* Grange Books, London

WOLFE, Art and DE LA TORRE, Julio 1990 *Owls - Their Life and Behaviour* Crown, New York

YAMAMOTO, Sumio 1999 *The Blakiston's Fish Owl* The Hokkaido Shimbun Press, Japan (*Text in Japanese*)

OWLS Journeys around the world

OPPOSITE
The piercing eyes of an
Australian Barking Owl.
A possible subject for the
next journey.

Index

Main accounts including photographs – **Bold Type**

Photographs – *Italics*

All others – Normal Type

Ant,Yellow Crazy *Anoplolepis gracilipes* 97

Aspinall,Peter 102

Bee-eater,Carmine *Merops nubicoides* 203

Bittern,Little *Ixobrychus minutus* 203

Blakiston,Thomas 143

Booby,Abbott's *Sula abbotti* 84,88

Bosunbird,Golden *Phaethon lepturus fulvus* 84

Buzzard,Common *Buteo buteo* 59,68,74

Capercaillie *Tetrao urogallus* 137,138,*139*

Cockatoo,White *Cacatua galerita* 188,228

Cowan,Alan 16,*23*,26,144,*153*

Cowan,Susan 16

Crab,Christmas Island Red *Gecarcoidea natalis* 84,88,*89*

Crab,Costa Rica Red *sp?* 101,102,*103*

Crab,Robber *Birgus latro* 89,91

Crane,Japanese *Grus japonensis* 156,*158*

Crow,Jungle *Corvus macrorhynchos* 148

Cuckoo,Brush *Cacomantis variolosus* 198

Currawong,Pied *Strepera graculina* 228

Curry-Lindahl, Kai 19

Deer,Shika 152

Demetrio *108*,109,110

Drongo,Fork-tailed *Dicrurus adsimilis* 209

Drongo,Spangled *Dicrurus bracteatus* 209

Falcon,Saker *Falco cherrug* 59

Fieldfare *Turdus pilaris* 137

Flentje,Bill 216-231,*217*

Flycatcher,Lemon-breasted *Microeca flavigaster* 198

Forsman,Eric *168*,169-175,*173*

Frey,Hans 59,60,*64*,67,68,71,74,77

Frigatebird,Christmas Island *Fregata andrewsi* 84,85

Galah *Cacatua roseicapella* 228

Gibbons,Dale 216,217,219,220

Glider,Sugar *Petaurus breviceps* 228

Goose,White-fronted *Anser albifrons* 25,28

Goshawk,Christmas Island *Accipiter fasciatus natalis* 94,96,97

Hedgehog *Erinaceus europaeus* 64,65,68

Heron,White-faced *Ardea novaehollandiae* 83

Hill,Richard 84,87,94

Hobby *Falco subbuteo* 59

Hollands, Margaret 16,26,30,34,41,42,101,105,109,115,126

Hollands,Richard 46

Holt,Denver 15,16,19,30,33,34,38

Honeyeater,Fuscous *Lichenostomus fuscus* 224

Honeyeater,Graceful *Meliphaga gracilis* 198

Honeyeater,White-plumed *Lichenostomus penicillatus* 224

Honeyeater,Yellow *Lichenostomus flavus* 224

Jaeger,Arctic *Stercorarius parasiticus* 21

Jaeger,Long-tailed *Stercorarius longicaudus* 21

Jaeger,Pomarine *Stercorarius pomarinus* 21

Jay *Garrulus glandarius* 68

Kestrel,Common *Falco tinnunculus* 59,74

Kestrel,Nankeen *Falco cenchroides* 83

Kite,Black *Milvus migrans* 59

Kite,Black-shouldered *Elanus notatus* 38

Kite,Swallow-tailed *Elanoides forficatus* 104,105

Lammergeyer *Gypaetus barbatus* 59,60,72-74,*73*,*77*

Lemming *Lemmus sp.* 15,16,30,33,34,38

Longspur,Lapland *Calcarius lapponicus* 38

Loon,Pacific *Gavia pacifica* 25,33

Loon,Red-throated *Gavia stellata* 33

Loschl,Pete 171,*173*

Magpie *Pica pica* 137

Magpie,Australian *Gymnorhina tibicen* 228

Monkey,Howler 109

Monkey,Squirrel 102

Motmot,Turquoise-browed *Eumomota superciliosa* 104,106

Nightjar,Large-tailed *Caprimulgus macrurus* 197

Nighthawk *Chordeiles minor* 175

Oldsquaw *Clangula hyemalis* 19

Osprey *Pandion haliaetus* 115

Owl,Barking *Ninox connivens* 94

Owl,Barn *Tyto alba* **9-11**,59,60,109,179

Owl,Barred *Strix varia* 165

Owl,Black and White *Strix nigrolineata* 110

Owl,Blakiston's Fish *Ketupa blakistoni* **142-161**,215

Owl,Boobook *Ninox novaeseelandiae* 88,91,94,191

Owl,Buffy Fish *Bubo ketupu* 143

Owl,Burrowing *Athene cunicularia* **46-55**

Owl,Christmas Island Hawk *Ninox natalis* **82-97**

Owl,European Eagle *Bubo bubo* 41,**58-77**,137,143,147,203,210,215

Owl,European Pygmy *Glaucidium passerinum* 119,130-132,*133,134*

Owl,European Scops *Otus scops* 130

Owl,Ferruginous Pygmy *Glaucidium brasilianum* *108*,109

Owl,Great Grey *Strix nebulosa* 135-137,*136*,159

Owl,Lesser Sooty *Tyto multipunctata* **178-191**

Owl,Little *Athene noctua* 48,60

Owl,Long-eared *Asio otus* 59,74,76

Owl,Masked *Tyto novaehollandiae* 188

Owl,Moluccan Hawk *Ninox squamipila* 94

Owl,Oriental Hawk *Ninox scutulata* 94

Owl,Pacific Screech *Otus cooperi* *106,107*,107

Owl,Pel's Fishing *Scotopelia peli* 143,203

Owl,Powerful *Ninox strenua* 72,94,197,**214-231**

Owl,Rufous *Ninox rufa* 88,94,102,105,**192-199**,217,224

Owl,Short-eared *Asio flammeus* 25,59

Owl,Snowy *Nyctea scandiaca* **15-43**

Owl,Sooty *Tyto tenebricosa* 152,179,191

Owl,Spectacled *Pulsatrix perspicillata* **100-111**

Owl,Spotted Eagle *Bubo africanus* **202-207**

Owl,Spotted *Strix occidentalis* **164-175**

Owl,Tawny *Strix aluco* 59,60,119

Owl,Tengmalm's *Aegolius funereus* *118*,119,*128*,130,*131,132*

Owl,Ural *Strix uralensis* 38,**115-138**,*158*,159

Owl,Verreaux's Eagle *Bubo lacteus* 203,**209-11**,215

Owl,White-faced Scops *Ptilopsis granti* **204,208-9**,*211*

Pacheco,Oscar Gonzales 105,106

Partridge,Common *Perdix perdix* 68

Pauraque,Common *Nyctidromus albicollis* 110

Petersen,Julie 19,21,22,30

Phalarope,Red *Phalaropus fulicaria* *18*,19

Phalarope,Red-necked *Phalaropus lobatus* 19

Pintail *Anas acuta* 19,38

Pitta,Buff-breasted *Pitta versicolor* 198

Plover,Golden *Pluvialis dominica* 25,34

Poiku,Pekka 137

Possum,Brush-tailed *Trichosurus vulpecula* 220,229

Possum,Ring-tailed *Pseudochirus peregrinus* 220,227,229

Pygmy-possum *Cercatetus sp.*188

Rabbit *Oryctolagus cuniculus* 228

Ranowsky,Gustavo 47,53

Raven,Australian *Corvus coronoides* 228

Raven,Common *Corvus corax* 28

Sandpiper,Pectoral *Calidris melanotus* 19,*21*

Sandpiper,Semi-palmated *Calidris pusilla* 19,34

Saurola,Hemuli 137,*138*

Saurola,Pertti 15,*114*,115-137,*127*,143

Scrubfowl,Orange-footed *Megapodius reinwardt* 188

Sea-eagle,Steller's *Haliaeetus pelagicus* 156,*157*,159

Seidensticker,Matt 34,38

Soderquist,Todd 229

Söllner,Fred 60,*61*,67,74-77

Steyn,Peter 203,*205*,210

Stone-curlew,Bush *Burhinus grallarius* 152,197

Suydam,Robert 15,30

Swan,Tundra *Cygnus columbianus* 24-25,25

Swan,Whooper *Cygnus Cygnus* 145,*146*,147

Takata,Masaru and Sako 144

Thrush, Christmas Island *Turdus poliocephalus erythropleurus* 96

Thrush,Varied *Ixoreus naevius* 172

Ulla 115,129

Vulture,Griffon *Gyps fulvus* 74

Waterhen,White-breasted *Amaurornis phoenicurus* 83

Watkins,Rob 216,219

Wigeon,American *Anas americana* 19

Woodpecker,Hoffmann's *Melanerpes hoffmannii* 108

Wren,Winter *Troglodytes troglodytes* 169

Yamamoto,Sumio 143-160

Young,John *180*,183-191,193

Zuniga,Agustin 101

First published in Australia in 2004 by

BLOOMINGS
BOOKS

Bloomings Books
Melbourne, Australia
Phone +61 (0)3 9427 1234
Facsimile +61 (0) 3 9427 9066
sales@bloomings.com.au

Bloomings Books is a specialist publisher and
Distributor of horticultural and natural history books.

The publisher would welcome readers' comments:
warwick@bloomings.com.au

Designed by: Danie Pout Design
Principal Photographer: David Hollands
Publisher: Warwick Forge

National Library of Australia, Cataloguing-in-publication entry:

Hollands, David, 1933-
Owls: journeys around the world.

Includes index.

ISBN 1 876473 50 9.

1. Owls. 2. Strigidae 3. Tytonidae. I. Title.

598.97